# The Visitor's Guide
## to
## CRETE

# THE VISITOR'S GUIDE TO CRETE

## FIONA BULMER

MPC

HUNTER
PUBLISHING INC

Published by:
Moorland Publishing Co Ltd,
Moor Farm Road,
Airfield Estate,
Ashbourne,
Derbyshire DE6 1HD
England

British Library Cataloguing in
Publication Data:
Bulmer, Fiona
   The visitor's guide to Crete
   1. Greece. Crete - Visitor's guides
   I. Title
   914.9980446

ISBN 0 86190 388 9 (paperback)

Published in the USA by:
Hunter Publishing Inc,
300 Raritan Center Parkway,
CN 94, Edison, NJ 08818
ISBN 1 55650 274 5 (USA)

Cover photograph:
MPC Picture Collection.

Illustrations have been supplied as
follows: MPC Picture Collection:
pp 15 (both), 18, 23, 26, 30, 34, 79,
83, 87, 90, 94, 102, 103, 110 (top),
111, 114, 115, 118, 119 (both), 122-
23, 139, 142, 143 (both), 146, 155,
158, 159, 163 (both), 166, 167, 190,
195, 199, 203, 206.

All other illustrations are from the
author.

Colour and black & white
origination by:
Scantrans, Singapore

Printed in the UK by:
Richard Clay Ltd, Bungay, Suffolk

# *CONTENTS*

| | | |
|---|---|---|
| Acknowledgements | | 7 |
| Introduction | | 8 |
| 1 | Eastern Crete | 36 |
| 2 | Iraklion to Ayios Nikolaos | 56 |
| 3 | Iraklion | 76 |
| 4 | South of Iraklion | 96 |
| 5 | Iraklion to Rethimnon | 124 |
| 6 | Rethimnon | 135 |
| 7 | South of Rethimnon | 147 |
| 8 | Rethimnon to the Akrotiri Peninsula | 164 |
| 9 | Hania | 174 |
| 10 | Western Crete | 187 |
| | Tips For Travellers | 208 |
| | Further Information for Visitors | 232 |
| | Index | 250 |

## Key to Symbols Used in Text Margin and on Maps

 Recommended walk

 Archaeological site

 Nature reserve/Animal interest

 Garden

 Mosque

 Cave

 Church/Ecclesiastical site

 Building of interest

 Castle/Fortification

 Museum/Art gallery

 Beautiful view/Scenery, Natural phenomenon

 Other place of interest

 Sailing

## Key to Maps

——— Minor Roads

═══ Main Roads

⌇ River

 Town/City

● Town/Village

 Lake

# *ACKNOWLEDGEMENTS*

The author would like to thank Robert and Mary Bulmer and Richard Hurford for their help in the research and writing of this book.

# INTRODUCTION

T he island of Crete, known in Greek as Kriti, has two features
which distinguish it from most of the other mainstream holiday
resorts in the Mediterranean; its ancient history and its mountains.
Neither of these can be ignored, even by the most ardent seeker after
sun, sand and sea.

It is the fifth largest island in the Mediterranean; a long and thin
land mass, measuring 250km (155miles) in length. It varies in width
from 14km ($8^1/_2$ miles) at its narrowest point to 61km (38miles) at its
widest. However, distances on the island can be deceptive. The
British archaeologist, John Pendlebury, who travelled extensively on
the island, declared, 'Distances are useless. Times alone matter'. In
his book, he sticks closely to this criterion, pointing out that from
Ierapetra to Ano Viannos took 8 or 9 hours on foot. The reliabilty of
this form of measurement is somewhat undermined by the footnote
advising 'As to this time I am not certain, as I lost my way. 'All of this
will have a familiar ring to those who have attempted to travel about
the island; in this respect, little has changed in 60 years.

The mountains which cover two thirds of the 8,350km² (5,177sq
miles) surface area are the central cause of these problems. This
means that even today, when the road network is reasonably extensive, large parts of Crete remain inaccessible and the influence of
tourism in these areas can be surprisingly limited. Despite this, the
tourist industry is the most important source of revenue for the
island's economy and nearly one and a half million people visit Crete
each year.

The population of 502,000 lives mainly along the north coast, for
obvious geographical reasons. It is here that most of the holiday

resorts can be found although development is spreading to the south coast and into the west. Despite the length of coastline, much of it is too rocky to be accessible and there are very few safe ports. Only Kali Limines and Loutro provide safe, year-round anchorages on the south coast.

In the north, apart from the fine natural harbour at Souda Bay, only Iraklion and Sitia can accept large ships. This difficult geography has been encountered at first hand by many illustrious visitors, ranging from Menelaus to Saint Paul, who have been shipwrecked on the island.

There are really only two cities of any size; Iraklion, the capital and Hania, the former capital, with populations of 100,000 and 50,000 respectively. Rethimnon, Ierapetra and Sitia are medium sized towns but most of the population still live in villages either along the coast or in the mountains. In fact, half of the island's workforce is still directly employed in agriculture.

The island is divided into four prefectures, also known as *nomes*; Hania, Rethimnon, Iraklion and Lasithi; each with an administrative capital and further subdivided into provinces.

The prefecture of Hania covers the western part of the island which is the most mountainous and least developed region. The Levka Ori Mountains make much of the area inaccessible and there are several villages, like Loutro on the south coast, which can only be reached by boat or on foot.

The Samaria Gorge which runs through these mountains is the longest gorge in Europe and attracts thousands of visitors every year as one of the island's most spectacular natural landmarks.

The region also has two of the best beaches on the island at Elafonisi and Falasarna, with clear, turquoise water and bright, white sand. They may be difficult to reach but are all the more unspoiled for their isolated setting.

Looking at a map of the region, the visitor can hardly fail to notice the two fingers of land protruding from the far west of the island. These are the Rodopou and Gramvousa Peninsulas which are totally uninhabited; in fact, the Gramvousa Peninsula has never been inhabited. The Rodopou does have an ancient temple at its northern end but both peninsulas remain truly wild and remote places.

The prefecture of Rethimnon has the smallest area and lies at one of the narrowest parts of the island with the attractive Venetian town of Rethimnon as its capital. The region covers some of the high peaks

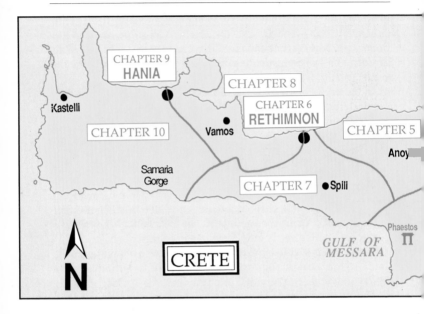

of the Psiloritis or Ida Range but is characterised more by lower hills and lush valleys. The finest of these is the Amari Valley, a quiet, peaceful region where traditional farming techniques are still much in evidence and the villages seem almost untouched by modern life. This is something of a false impression as the valley was the centre of much resistance during the German occupation and suffered many reprisals as a result.

On the south coast there are newer resorts which have grown out of fishing villages like Ayia Galini or Plakias and never quite lose their charm, whatever the ravages of tourist development.

The largest prefecture is that of Iraklion, covering an area of 2,641km² (1,637sq miles) and home to half the island's population. While the province straddles the highest mountain range on the island, it has more flat land than elsewhere, with the fertile Messara Plain stretching across the south, promoting settlement and prosperity. This prosperity is augmented by the tourist resorts along the northern shore east of Iraklion. Although they are not necessarily the most attractive places, these resorts remain highly popular.

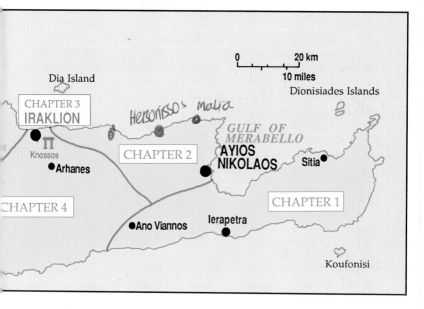

The region is well-known for its Minoan sites which include the Palace of *Knossos* and the lesser known Palace of *Phaestos*. The region's history is even more extensive than this, with a major Roman settlement at *Gortyn* and the Venetian walls around Iraklion itself.

At the eastern end of the island is Lasithi which is named after the plateau found on its western edge. Its capital is the resort of Ayios Nikolaos. This region has the whole range of attractions; a Minoan palace at *Zakros*, offshore islands with a long history like Spinalonga, and beautiful beaches. The far east is almost as undeveloped as the west and there are still few roads in this area.

The south-east coast is not as attractive as some of the other parts of the island, not least because of the intensive use of plastic greenhouses by farmers in search of a higher crop yield. For spectacular views, the best option is the drive along the north coast towards Sitia. This is known as the Cretan Riviera, where the road climbs high into the cliffs and looks down onto the deep blue of the Mediterranean below.

# Geography

The geographical position of the island has always been important and the greatest influence on its history. As the gateway to Greece and the Aegean on one side — Athens is only 175km (108 miles) away — and Africa on the other, the island has always been seen as a prize by those powers wishing to dominate the region. This accounts for its turbulent history of occupation by foreign forces.

It has never been an easy prize to capture though, with the mountains again crucial to the nature of the place. They provide ideal conditions within which a resistance movement can operate and the harsh life of the mountains seems to act as a breeding ground for the partisan spirit.

There are three main mountain ranges running the length of the island to form a spine broken in three places. In the far west are the Levka Ori or White Mountains, the highest peak being Pahnes, at 2,452m (8,042ft). In the centre is the Ida or Psiloritis Range with Mount Ida at 2,456m (8,056ft) just gaining the title of the highest summit. In the east is the Dikte Range which reaches a height of 2,148m (7,045ft). At the very eastern end of the island are the lower hills of the Sitia Range at around 1,000m (3,000ft) and there are 57 peaks over 2,000m (6,000ft), many of which are covered in snow throughout the winter.

Within these ranges there are several fertile upland plains. That of Lasithi, at a height of 850m (2,796ft), is the best-known and the only one that is inhabited all the year round. Others include the Nidha and Omalos Plateaux, the latter lies at the head of the Samaria Gorge. It is another distinctive feature of the Cretan landscape, claiming to be the longest gorge in Europe and one of several impressive ravines on the island. These plains are used for summer grazing and the cultivation of potatoes but in winter they are usually covered in snow.

The most fertile area of the island, only about 30 per cent of which allows for farming, is the Messara Plain which leads down to the south coast, a traditionally prosperous area and the site of many ancient settlements. It is fed by rivers running off the mountains, enjoys the hotter climate of the south and therefore supports the cultivation of a large number of crops that cannot be grown anywhere else.

The staple crops produced on the island are the same today as they have been since ancient times; olives and grapes. The trees of the former crop can be seen all over Crete in even the most barren landscapes; there are an estimated 13 million olive trees on the island. In summer these are surrounded by black plastic netting (a labour saving device) to harvest the olives as they fall. The olive is still the staple crop for many families and the harvest a communal activity. Each village has its own olive press from which not only the principal yield of the oil emerges, but also the ingredients for soap, animal feed and even a kind of fuel is extracted from the stones.

Crete exports 10,000 tonnes of sultanas every year and produces 25 per cent of Greek olive oil and 12 per cent of its wine. There are also extensive citrus groves and, with the arrival of plastic greenhouses, tomatoes and bananas are now grown all over the island.

Fruit is plentiful throughout the year, the variety depending on the season. The summer visitor is sure to see melons for sale piled high in mounds at the side of the road. Other fruits include the quince which is thought to have originated in Crete; its Latin name, *Cydonia*, reflects the ancient name of Hania and quince jam is available in many supermarkets.

There are over eight hundred farming villages where life remains undeniably difficult and poverty persists although it is a less obvious poverty than the urban squalor of other countries. It is clear that village life will have to change as depopulation continues and the traditional but slow agricultural techniques are superseded. It is already not uncommon to find abandoned villages where the population has left crumbling houses and gone to look for more prosperous employment in the towns.

Architecturally, the villages can be a disappointment. There is a real mixture of styles; the ubiquitous half-built building with reinforced concrete rods and a staircase leading nowhere seems to typify Cretan attitudes. Despite all this and the appalling roads which run through them (villagers have to pay for the upkeep of roads within the village), they retain a charm, an other-worldliness symptomatic of a very different culture which is both frustrating and enthralling for the visitor. Greece may now be part of the EEC but it is still in many respects closer to Byzantium.

## Climate

High temperatures and almost guaranteed summer sunshine are the characteristic features of the island's climate, bringing with it the subsequent problem of water shortages. Only five rivers never dry up and the summer visitor is much more likely to encounter dry river beds than hear the sound of rushing water.

It is unlikely to rain between May and September although there can be heavy rain in October and the winter can be surprisingly bleak. Claims that suntans can be obtained in late October should be treated with some scepticism and for much of the winter the high mountains are covered in snow.

There are several peculiarities to the Cretan climate which are worth noticing. The most significant one for the summer visitor is that the island is notoriously windy. July and August are known for the Meltemi, a north-west wind which moderates temperatures, making the sea rough, and sitting on the beach can be unpleasant; this should be borne in mind when planning the timing of a visit.

There are other winds which periodically plague the island, including one which blows off the desert and is likened to the Mistral for its adverse effect on the mood of the residents. The mountains are the other moderating factor on the weather. The higher ground is obviously cooler and has more rain but also has the interesting effect of blocking one side of the island's weather from the other. This can mean an unpleasant day on the northern coast may be fine and sunny on the southern side. There are, in any case, regional variations in climate; the south coast is warmer than the north and the east windier but drier than the west.

## Plant and Animal Life

Despite the lack of rain, the landscape can be unexpectedly lush with a profusion of flowers in spring. There are over 1,500 plant varieties on the island, including twenty species of orchid, and even in summer the oleanders still bloom and the water shortage does not seem to affect the colourful gardens that proliferate in many villages.

The hills are known for their scent which emanates not only from the purple heather on the high mountains but also from a large number of naturally growing herbs, including thyme and Cretan Dittany. The latter is a sort of wild marjoram which is highly prized as an aphrodisiac. It is also claimed to have powers to cure a variety of ills and Virgil relates a story of how Aeneas' mother travelled to Crete in order to find this plant to treat an arrow-wound her son had received.

Of course spring is the best time for the visitor with an interest in botany. This season offers the chance to see a profusion of wild

*There are many colourful plants to be found on Crete*

flowers including numerous orchids and anenomes. The mountains present an almost Alpine outlook; asphodel and iris are common, with one species (*Iris Cretica*) particular to the island, this flower has an orange stripe on its blue petals. Spring also offers the spectacular picture of almost every field standing out scarlet, covered in a carpet of poppies.

The fruit trees have their spring blossom and distinctive scent from the white almond blossom of February to the flowers of the orange and lemon trees a few months later. There will always be the more unusual sights too; a huge cactus standing in the middle of a lush mountain valley or a lone date palm on the coast.

In ancient times, the whole island was covered in forest but extensive deforestation has taken place, partly to provide the material to build ships required by the various occupying forces. This depletion led to changes in the climate and is one of the reasons for the barren nature of much of the land which is now covered in rather spiky undergrowth. This is only suitable for goats, whose grazing exacerbates the situation.

Apart from the ubiquitous donkeys and goats, the island's wildlife includes several kinds of lizard such as the brightly coloured, Balkan green lizard which can be over 1m (3ft) in length. There is one poisonous snake, despite the Cretans' claim that St Titus rid the island of all poisonous reptiles. The visitor, though, is more likely to see the grisly end of such creatures on the road than have any encounters with live ones.

The wild mountain goat, a sort of ibex which has various names, including agrimi or kri-kri, is the rarest animal on Crete but is now mainly kept in specially created offshore sanctuaries or in the Samaria Gorge Park to try and prevent its total extinction.

Birdlife is extensive on the island with griffon vultures common in the mountains as well the rarer Eleonora's falcon and numerous varieties of warblers. Driving along the roads in summer, one is likely to be accompanied by the wheeling and diving of the swallows and occasionally see the yellow flash of a goldfinch. All too often, these can be heard plaintively singing in cages outside souvenir shops. Crete is also the stopping off point for large numbers of migrating birds which tend to gather round any freshwater they can find; keen ornithologists should time their trips to coincide with this migration.

# Geology

The island has never been the subject of a systematic geological survey but it seems to have originally been linked to Asia and Europe before breaking away. Large numbers of fossils have been found on the island which substantiate this theory. It consists of a limestone spine of mountains which has facilitated the formation of over 2,000 caves, many of which have archaeological or historical interest. There are few mineral deposits on the island and much of the metal used in Minoan times was imported. There were, however, extensive gypsum quarries; a stone which was widely used in the Palace of *Knossos*.

Periodic severe earthquakes are the main geological curiosity of the island and are calculated to occur at least twice every century. They have necessitated frequent rebuilding of all the island's monuments, from Minoan times until the last major earthquake in 1926, and led one Venetian ruler to write home in 1508 of 'hideous roarings' coming from the earth. Minor tremors are much more frequent and cause little concern.

The volcanic island of Santorini is still active and many believe it was an eruption here that brought about the end of Minoan civilisation, calculating that any such eruption would have been many times more powerful than that of Krakatoa and the resultant tidal waves could have devastated Crete. These days, Santorini is much calmer and the destination for numerous day trips for tourists.

# Art and Literature

The earliest and best-known examples of Cretan art are the frescoes found in the Minoan palaces, now displayed in Iraklion Museum. These much restored pictures not only give valuable insights into Minoan culture and life but are held to display a fine artistic sense.

The frescoes never depict military scenes; this has been seen as suggesting that the Minoans lived in peaceful times, unlike many of their warring contemporaries. They also depict people and the fresco called *La Parisienne* is one of the first examples of portrait painting. Many subjects are naturalistic, such as that found at the villa of *Ayia Triadha* which showed a cat about to pounce on wild birds; others, like that from *Amnissos*, show flowers, in this case lilies.

Minoan sculpture is also held in high regard. One of the finest examples is the ivory bull leaper found at *Knossos* which is so

*Traditional transport*

delicately carved it seems that every sinew is outlined. The pottery showed highly developed skills too; so, although the Minoans did not leave any literary account of their life like their Classical descendants, they compensated for this by the extent and artistry of their pictorial creations.

The painting tradition re-emerged in the Byzantine era, now the frescoes were painted on the walls of the hundreds of churches which are scattered all around the island. It was religion that inspired these painters and the subjects are taken from the Bible. The Nativity, Baptism, Last Supper and Crucifixion became almost standard scenes and can be seen in virtually every church.

The Venetian period brought about a real upsurge in this kind of painting of icons and frescoes. The style changed, becoming more cosmopolitan and a Cretan School of icon painters emerged who were known throughout Europe where they often travelled after learning their skills at the academy of Ayia Ekaterini in Iraklion. One of the most famous icon painters of this period was Damaskinos. His icons can be seen in Ayia Ekaterini which is now a museum of religious art.

Some of the best frescoes are found in the church of Panayia Kera near Ayios Nikolaos in the east of the island. These are well-preserved and have scenes from the lives of the Virgin, and Christ as well as some of the Second Coming. They are interesting because they have examples both of the early, primitive style and the later, more sophisticated, painting.

Another fine icon is that found in the Toplou Monastery called *Lord Thou art Great* which depicts, in minute detail, hundreds of scenes from the Orthodox liturgy.

The best-known Cretan painter was Domenicos Theotokopoulos, otherwise known as El Greco. He was born in 1541 either in the village of Fodhele, near Iraklion, or in Iraklion itself. He may have studied at Ayia Ekaterini before leaving the island for Spain where he painted most of his work.

It is here that the Cretan artisitic tradition seems to have stopped and it must be said that it was never particularly extensive in range. This is particularly true of the religious and stylised nature of the island's early art.

*Locals Bailing Straw*

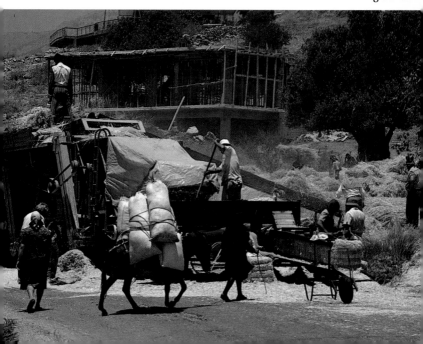

While the Classical Greeks left behind a whole range of literary works, Crete remained something of a backwater in this field, having to be content with the references made to the island by illustrious writers like Homer rather than producing a chronicler of its own.

It was not until the Venetian period that any literature of note was produced on the island, with drama seeing something of a revival. Two plays which have survived are occasionally performed today; *Gyparis*, a pastoral comedy, and *Erophile*, a tragedy, both of which owe much to Classical drama.

The most famous work of this period was the epic poem, *Erotokritos*, written in 1646 by Vincenzos Kornaros. It tells the story at great length of frustrated love between Erotokritos and Aretousa which finally triumphs after many setbacks. Despite being written in rather obscure Cretan idiom, it was adopted by villagers who learn it off by heart and then sing it. Whatever the literary merits of the poem, it has become an integral part of Cretan heritage.

It took two centuries for Crete to come up with another writer of any international repute; Nikos Kazantzakis, whose works include *Zorba the Greek*, *Freedom and Death* and *The Last Temptation of Christ*. These works are written in a grand style, especially *Freedom and Death* which deals with resistance to the Turks. The subject is the fierce fighter, the grand gesture of duty which always leads to tragedy and death.

While Crete still influences international cultural and artistic life, it is not the written tradition that is important on the island but the oral folk tradition of song and dance.

## Culture, Religion and Myths

In the mountain villages, the visitor will have a strong sense of a timeless tradition which is untouched by modern life; donkeys are still one of the main means of transport; the men seem to spend most of their time in the *kafeinon* clicking worry beads while black-clad women do all the work. Many of the farming techniques are antiquated and implements like the wine press found in the Minoan villa at Vathipetro bear striking similarities to those used today.

Of course, in the towns, especially those which are holiday resorts, the way of life is very different but even here it is possible that the visitor will catch a glimpse of the old traditions and the urban residents are certain to maintain their ties with 'the village'.

A certain conservatism is claimed for the Cretans and they are said to be offended by what they perceive as loose morals on the part of tourists. However, topless bathing is definitely the norm and nudists can find numerous beaches where they are tolerated, although the police do object from time to time. Little of this conservatism is apparent in the major holiday resorts. However, a certain reserve on the part of the older generation of Cretans may be the price paid for years of hooligan behaviour by certain young visitors.

The culture and folklore traditions of the island are closely related to those of mainland Greece and the plate-throwing evenings of dance and Bazouki music are those offered to the tourists. However, the island does have a rich collection of epic songs and poems of its own, detailing the heroic struggles of the islanders against the occupying forces. These centre around the *palikari*, the archetypal fierce man of the mountains who is felt to epitomise the Cretan characteristics of resistance and willingness to fight to the death for liberty.

The distinctive song of Crete is called the *Mantinada* and consists of rhyming couplets either improvised or repeated from the repertoire built up through history and passed on through the generations. They are essentially love songs but cover the whole range of human emotions in grand, dramatic style.

Traditional dances can have a very long history with extensive depiction of dancing on Minoan pottery and the instruction for Dedalus to build a dance floor for Ariadne, Minos' daughter, described by Homer. Many of these dances are still performed today and displays of dancing are an integral part of the numerous summer festivals held in the major towns.

Weddings and saints' days are the best times to experience the true folklore of Crete. Up in the villages, these celebrations turn into festivals with music, dancing, plentiful food and wine — all held in the street with the whole village participating.

All this may suggest a gentle pace of life but this has not always been the case. The Cretans have long had a fearsome reputation as fighters and were much sought after as mercenaries for foreign wars, even in ancient times. That ferocity was much magnified in the resistance against those who occupied Crete itself, as the invaders found to their cost. No occupying power has managed to totally subdue the native population and this history of the rebellions is central to the culture and traditions of the island. This is reflected in the numerous holidays, like Arkhadi Day or Independence Day, which commemorate this resistance.

Everywhere on the island, there are reminders of the Greek Orthodox faith, one of the earliest forms of Christianity which owed its allegiance to Byzantium, not Rome. The faith goes unquestioned and the priest is still the centre of a village, playing a secular as well as a sacred role. This is, perhaps, precisely because religion is such an accepted part of everyday life, often accompanied by a belief in miracles and the mystical powers of holy relics. The priest has always been active in politics and particularly in the revolts against the various occupying forces, when the monasteries were centres of resistance. The Cretan clergy have never been afraid of being directly involved in the battle.

There are churches and chapels everywhere on the island, the earliest dating from the sixth century and the latest still in the process of being built. New church building is clearly a major industry and it is much easier to find the money to build a new church than a new health centre; even small villages may have two or three churches.

Another curiosity the visitor may notice are the numerous shrines in the form of miniature chapels by the side of the road. These are usually dedicated to a particular saint and it is still customary for travellers to stop, pray and make an offering. This can be in the form of a lighted candle, often to ensure a safe journey which, considering the state of Cretan roads, may well be a good idea. Also visible both here and in churches are small metal plates on which a part of the body is depicted. This is a long-standing tradition, intended to bring about the cure of that particular afflicted part.

Many people consider Crete to be more Greek than Greece itself and since ancient times it has taken an importance on itself, not least in the myths associated with it. Crete itself was supposed to be a nymph and the mother of Pasiphae. However, its central claim is that it was the birthplace of Zeus, although the precise cave where this event took place is still disputed. He was then suckled by the goat nymph Amalthia and protected by the Kouretes warriors. *Gortyn* is supposedly the site of his marriage to Europa and, most unfortunately for an immortal god, his burial site is on Mount Iouktas.

Minos, the legendary and maybe real King of Crete, was the son of Zeus and Europa. From these origins a tangled story emerges which includes the history of the Minotaur, (the progeny of Minos' wife Pasiphae's predilection for bulls) and, beyond this, the coming of Theseus to kill the monster and its tragic implications for Minos'

*The locals are very friendly towards visitors*

daughters Ariadne and Phedra. His other daughter, Akakallis, was also a nymph who was loved by Apollo and associated with *Tarra*, now Ayia Roumeli, on the south coast.

Dedalus and Icarus were supposed to have taken off on their ill-fated flight from Crete; Dedalus having been Minos' chief engineer. He was exiled because of the way the minotaur story ended — Ariadne running away with Theseus. Much later, Homer was talking of the 'Great Island' in the 'wine dark sea' and Minos taking counsel with Zeus every 9 years. All this gave the island a sense of being at the centre of things; something which does not persist today.

## History of the Island
The history of the island is so extensive it cannot be escaped. Even in the most pre-packaged, undistinguished holiday resorts, there can be a Minoan palace just down the road, a Roman fish tank in the harbour or a Venetian fountain in the square.

Crete has always presented difficulties for archaeologists because its most significant finds pre-date Classical sources. As no corroboration can be gained from these, virtually all of what is known about Minoan civilisation has been gained from interpretation of artefacts uncovered by excavation. It is hard to believe now, but the existence of the Minoan civilisation had been unsuspected until the discoveries at *Knossos* early this century.

The earliest indications of settlement on Crete come from the Neolithic period (about 6000BC) with remains of pottery found on sites around the island, especially in caves but also at all the famous Minoan palaces. These people were probably hunter gatherers who originated from Anatolia.

The British archaeologist Arthur Evans, who excavated *Knossos*, called the Bronze Age in Crete the Minoan period, after King Minos. He then split this period into Early Minoan, Middle Minoan and Late Minoan, each of these being further subdivided ie; Early Minoan I, Early Minoan II, Early Minoan III. This labelling is widely used although the exact dates separating these periods are still disputed as the dating can only be made by examining different styles of pottery and any division is bound to be arbitrary and open to argument. Roughly speaking, Early Minoan covers the period 2500-1950BC; Middle Minoan 1950-1550BC and Late Minoan 1550-1400BC.

There is another rival system of chronology devised by a Greek archaeologist, N. Platon, this falls into four periods; Pre-Palatial; Proto-Palatial, Neo-Palatial and Post-Palatial. The latter covers the period after the Minoan collapse in 1450BC and overlaps somewhat with Evans' Late Minoan period. The fact that the palaces cannot be dated with absolute accuracy, even carbon dating has proved ineffective, means that there is plenty of room for alternative and sometimes eccentric views to emerge on the subject.

There was a transition period between the Neolithic times and the Early Minoan or Pre-Palatial period from which a few tombs have been uncovered, along with the first remains of houses made of stone suggesting a growth of a more settled, urban society. The important sites in this period were found at *Vasiliki* and *Mirtos*, significant not for the quantity or quality of the finds but simply because they were so old. The pottery from *Vasiliki* has a distinctive, mottled style and shows an increase in sophistication. *Vasiliki* has been seen by some as a prototype for *Knossos* with an early palace structure discovered. At the palace sites themselves there is evidence of settlement during this period.

A significant date in the island's history was 1900BC; it marked the building of the first palaces at *Knossos*, *Phaestos*, Malia and *Zakros* and these are known as the old palaces. Various villas and whole towns, like *Gournia*, were also constructed and mark the development of a new and distinct urban culture indicating both political stability and prosperity. New styles of pottery date from this period including that called Kamares ware which is much finer than previous work and probably resulted from the use of a more sophisticated potter's wheel.

Much of this building was destroyed in 1700BC by an earthquake. This necessitated extensive rebuilding, usually on top of the originals. These later buildings are known as the new palaces and are, in substance, what we see today on the palace sites. This catastrophe does not seem to have disrupted life or culture and progress continued throughout this period.

The years up until 1450BC really marked the apogee of Minoan civilisation with clear power and prosperity; a period in which the arts flourished and the Minoans dominated the Aegean, becoming a seafaring nation. The Minoan fleet controlled the seas both militarily and commercially and some claim that their ships went as far as Scandinavia. Although this may be far fetched, they obviously had much influence on nearby islands and extensive trading links with

*The enterprising Cretans sell their wares to today's visitors*

places like Cyprus, from where they imported large quantities of copper.

Many outlines of Minoan society and culture have been put forward, some of which clearly indulge in romantic fantasies about the sophistication of the people. These were severely rocked by the discovery, 10 years ago at Anemospilia near Arhanes, of evidence that the Minoans indulged in human sacrifices. Minoan religion predates the Hellenic Gods and seems to have focused on a goddess who stood as some kind of mother earth figure with numerous depictions and figurines representing her. Other objects of worship include a snake cult and, apparently, some peasants still leave out milk and offerings for the snake goddess today.

Evidence for the nature of Minoan religion is particularly extensive from the numerous shrines found both in houses and in caves as well as the peak sanctuaries. Some of the most spectacular finds have come from tombs indicating a belief in an after life, hence all the possessions buried with the dead as well as offerings to the newly dead. However, it does seem that the living were not as generous to the dead as in the Egyptian culture of the same period.

It is particularly difficult to build up a picture of a society when so little literary evidence is available. Admittedly, tablets with Linear A script and Linear B script have been discovered. These are tablets with hieroglyphic writing inscribed on them and were found on the major sites. Linear B script is now accepted by most authorities to have been correctly deciphered by Michael Ventris as an early form of Greek. Many believe this shows that the influence of the mainland Greeks came to the island much earlier than was previously thought. The translation of the earlier Linear A script is still unclear, although some progress has been made by adapting the techniques of the later script to the earlier one. What has been deciphered turns out to be the Minoan equivalent of tax returns, simply listing the numbers of various objects and animals in the palace.

Much information can, however, be gained from the artefacts discovered. It is clear that the Minoans had an agriculture based economy with many tools found to confirm this; olives were a staple crop then as now, as were varieties of fruit and vegetables, honey and wine, some of which they probably exported.

The existence of the palaces clearly brought about a demand for more luxurious types of goods such as jewellery and new professions to serve this demand will have emerged. *Knossos* would certainly have required a whole army of fresco painters, sculptors and jewellers.

It seems the Minoans were a sporting nation; depictions of boxing and bull leaping are common and the fact that women participated in these suggests a certain equality between the sexes; this is further underlined by the depiction of females on vases and other works of art.

Bull leaping is a particularly interesting sport requiring great athleticism. The pictures indicate that the athlete had to vault onto the bull by seizing its horns and somersaulting over onto its back. The sport seems to have had a religious significance, perhaps accompanying a sacrifice. The bull was certainly a sacred animal widely depicted on the artefacts and perhaps associated with the Minotaur myth. The sport seems to have been peculiar to the Minoans for no convincing link can be drawn with Spanish bullfighting.

Evidence suggests that politically and culturally the Minoans were the predominant people in the region at the time but little is known of how they organised their own state. It could have been a single state led by *Knossos* and an all powerful priest king or a series of power bases around each palace. Whatever the system, it all collapsed in 1450BC when there was a great catastrophe which destroyed virtually all the Minoan constructions and brought their civilisation to an end. Although *Knossos* was not quite as badly damaged as the other palaces, it was completely destroyed 100 years later.

The nature of the catastrophe has not been established for certain and there are numerous conflicting theories. On one side, are those who believe there was some kind of natural disaster such as an earthquake or maybe a tidal wave in the aftermath of the volcanic explosion on the Island of Thera which is known to have taken place at this time. On the other side, are those who believe disaster came at the hands of an invading power like the Myceneaens, who came to dominate the mainland at this period and could reasonably be assumed to be in conflict with the Minoans. Pendlebury declares 'Everything points to a deliberate sacking on the part of enemies of the most powerful cities on Crete.' However, there is plenty of evidence to support the natural disaster theory, including large pieces of volcanic pumice found in the Palace of *Zakros*.

What is clear is that after the destruction of the palaces, the Myceneans settled on the island and sometimes re-occupied the remains of the Minoan settlements. The native Minoans, now called Eteocretans, retreated to small towns in the hills, like Karphi above the Lasithi Plateau where Minoan culture persisted, though on a smaller scale.

The Mycenean influence continued for about 200 years but, like all the Bronze Age civilisations, it was superseded, in this case by that of the Dorians. They created numerous city states on the island which were often at war with each other. There are many sites which contain remains of this period, although they are seldom very well-preserved.

However, yet again the science of archaeology fails to be definite, with some supporting a view that the Myceneans were there much earlier and produced all that has been attributed to the Minoans. Homer, in the *Odyssey*, complicates matters further by indicating that these events took place much later and that all the races were there at the same time; Dorians, Achaeans, Pelasgians as well as Minoans. However, this may simply be artistic licence of course.

There followed a rather dark period with the main progress occurring on mainland Greece while Crete remained out of this, preoccupied with internal affairs. However, the Dorians did have a strong social structure and some city states prospered and made alliances with each other and with foreign states. The famous Law Code found at *Gortyn* dates from 480BC and consists of twelve tablets and over 600 lines of legal guidelines. It is is one of the island's most important archaeological finds and gives extensive insights into the Classical society of that time, showing considerable sophistication in social organisation. To call this period the dark ages is, perhaps, a simplification of the situation.

The city states were often at war with each other and the Romans stepped in as peacemakers several times and then decided to take total control. After one failed attempt to capture the island, the Romans, led by Quintus Metellus, took over in 67BC although they continued to meet resistance from some of the city states. Their capital was at *Gortyn* but reminders of their presence are found in many regions of the island. It seems the island flourished, becoming a major trading centre and stopping off point for various travellers, including Hannibal and St Paul.

St Paul later decided Crete merited his attentions and sent St Titus to amend the Cretans' defective ways. He outlined these in a letter to Titus in which he repeated the prejudiced view of the period that

*A large cactus
provides shade from
the intense heat of the
sun*

'Cretans are always liars, evil beasts, lazy gluttons.'

On the division of the Roman Empire, Crete came under the control of Byzantium and reverted to being something of a backwater. However, it did not escape the attentions of the Arabs and, in AD824, a Saracen occupation centred around Iraklion began. They built a ditch around the city, called it *El Khandak* and made it a centre for piracy and slave trading.

This occupation lasted for over a century, surviving three attempts by the Byzantine Empire to regain control. The Arabs were finally defeated in AD961 by Nikopharus Phokas, whose attack on Iraklion included catapulting the heads of captured Muslims back into the city. This technique had the desired effect and Byzantine rule was restored.

A large number of churches date from this period which saw the increasing spread of Christianity. Many of these are still visible today, although not always in a good state of repair and the island is a rich ground for those with an interest in Byzantine art.

*Windmills at Seli Ambelou, south of Iraklion*

In 1204 the fourth crusade, which seems to have rampaged around the region, turned its attention to Constantinople and the Byzantine Empire began to collapse. A deal was struck with Venice under which Crete was handed over for a nominal fee.

The Venetian occupation was opposed by both their Italian rivals (the Genoese) and by the native population. The Genoese had several footholds on the island and captured Hania in 1263 but, despite this, the Venetians rapidly achieved a dominance and Crete prospered. The island was never peaceful and frequently disturbed by pirate raids led by Barbarossa. These devastated many of the coastal cities and led to the construction of the defensive fortresses and walls which dominate the island today.

The Venetians presided over a period of cultural renaissance. The Church, both Catholic and Orthodox, flourished; the Cretan school of icon painting became established and monasteries set up numerous schools which became well-known centres of learning. The epic poem *Erotokritos* was written in this period.

The native hatred for the occupying force may have been controlled but did not dissipate and revolts continued. In 1263 another uprising prompted the forced removal of the population from the Lasithi Plateau and it remained uninhabited for over a century, depriving the island of the produce of a rich, fertile region. Generally though, the Venetians managed the economy well and Cretan wines were widely exported and became famous throughout Europe.

The Turks of the Ottoman Empire had seen Crete as a target ever since their capture of Constantinople and their invasion began in 1645. They captured Hania immediately, with Rethimnon capitulating soon after. The attack on Iraklion proved to be a very different matter. The besieged city attracted international sympathy and supplies were sent in by sea. The French even sent a force of 7,000 men to help out but their leader, the Duke of Beaufort, was killed and the expedition abandoned. However, the Venetians fought on and it was 21 years before the invaders managed to force Iraklion to surrender after one of the longest sieges in history which cost well over 100,000 lives.

There were frequent revolts against the Turks, with the natural resentment against occupying forces being compounded by the difference of religion and the poverty resulting from economic mismanagement. By 1750, figures show that there were 60,000 Christians on the island and 200,000 Muslims. How many of these conversions were genuine and how many were merely a way of avoiding the punitive taxes levied on Christians is unclear.

The Turkish political system proved disastrous for the native population. Each region was ruled by *pashas*, who were usually corrupt and used their troops to further their own ends or, even worse, let the soldiers run wild. In sharp contrast to the Venetians, they constructed very few new buildings and left the existing ones to fall into disrepair.

The year 1770 saw the first major rebellion which was led by the Sfakian, Daskaloyiannis, who was inspired by Russian promises of help which turned out to be unfounded. The revolt then failed and the rebels were captured. Daskaloyiannis remained defiant and was skinned alive in Iraklion. The full story is told, undoubtedly with the addition of dramatic effects, in a folk poem *The Song of Daskaloyiannis*.

The revolutions gathered pace in the nineteenth century, with the uprising of 1821 being a response to the War of Independence on the Greek mainland. In 1828, Hadzi Michali Daliani acquired a ship and landed at Frangokastello where he waited for the Turks to attack, a typical insistence on the grand gesture of defiance rather than the militarily sensible option of heading into the mountains. The inevitable happened and the rebellion was crushed.

Then, in 1866, came the best-known and most symbolic insurrection of all which ended with the Cretan rebels blowing up the Arkhadi Monastery, killing the attackers and defenders alike. This was another typical act ensuring native martyrdom. The event attracted international attention from such diverse figures as Victor Hugo and Garibaldi.

Finally, in 1898, after further struggles, Independence under the Great Powers (France, Great Britain, Russia and Italy) was granted. The island was ruled by a High Commissioner; Prince George (the son of the Greek King) and, although this worked for a while, trouble soon flared again. In 1905, Eleftherios Venizelos, the Cretan politician, later to become Prime Minister of Greece, set up an alternative assembly demanding immediate union with Greece — riots and conflict ensued. These were only calmed by the resignation of Prince George and promises that union would eventually come. Finally, in 1913, *Enosis* (union with Greece) was achieved.

The turbulent political situation persisted, now affected by the mainland's problems. There was political instability throughout the Balkans which was not helped by Greek military adventurism on the Turkish mainland. This led to the final exodus of the remaining Turks on the island, under an acrimonious population exchange worked out between the two countries. Internal political problems persisted, with Venizelos, a committed republican, at their heart until his enforced exile by the monarchists.

Then, in 1941, the strategic position of the island made it central to the dominance of the Mediterranean during World War II and attracted the attention of both Hitler and Churchill. A German airborne attack by elite paratroopers was initially beaten back, except at Maleme in the west of the island. The lack of aircover for Allied troops and, some would claim, incompetent and unco-ordinated command led, after heavy fighting, to a failure to consolidate this initial success.

The counter attack at Maleme did not succeed, despite brave fighting by the New Zealanders, and led to the decision to evacuate the island. Even evacuation proved difficult; the Royal Navy suffered heavy losses trying to take men off the island while under airborne attack. The retreating troops needed all the help they could get from local partisans which came from all quarters, including .

*Crete provides sun & sea for todays holidaymaker*

shepherds and monks. The battle and the subsequent resistance are the subject of many books both by military historians and those who took part in the operation.

The German occupation lasted until 1944 and was strongly resisted by groups of locals based, as ever, in the mountains. The resistance continued, despite severe reprisals which included the burning of whole villages.

The most famous incident of this period was the abduction of the German commander on the island, General Kreipe, by a group of English agents; a rather literary bunch including Patrick Leigh-Fermor. The event is described by Stanley Moss in his book *Ill Met by Moonlight*. It was an incredible, amateurish attempt which succeeded despite frequent bungling which included the fact that to summon the boat to take them off the island they had to signal in morse code and no one in the party knew how to use it.

The war still haunts the island; there are memorials all over Crete and most poignant of all are the rows of graves in the war cemeteries at Souda and Maleme. The war is remembered in this way but forgotten by some when serving the huge numbers of German tourists who come to the island. There is a sense of irony in the fact that the visitor is sometimes as likely to be addressed by Cretans in German as in English.

Today Crete is very much part of the mainland political scene, although retaining a certain independence of spirit and a greater prosperity than much of Greece. It has no independent assembly but sends representatives directly to the Athens parliament and has a record of firm support for the PASOK socialist party. However, the west of the island is an exception to this trend and, given the fluid political situation in Greece, allegiances can swiftly change.

International interest in Crete still focuses on its ancient history rather than its current politics. Excavations which started in earnest at the beginning of this century with *Knossos* and *Phaestos* continue. Only 20 years ago, a previously unknown Minoan palace at *Zakros* was uncovered and the French, Italian and British schools are still very active. However, it is not the archaeologists who form the bulk of the foreign visitors but holidaymakers, mainly from Britain and Germany. This constitutes a different kind of occupation to the many already seen by the island and the first that has been encouraged rather than resisted.

# 1
# *EASTERN CRETE*

B eyond Ayios Nikolaos, the far east of the island can be surprisingly unspoilt. Dominated by the yellow tones of the Sitia
Mountains, a considerable part of this region is still inaccessible or at
least out of the reach of modern tourist development. The landscape
varies a great deal but there are few really fertile areas. Most of the
agriculture is devoted to olives although Sitia is known for its sultana
crop.

The mountains, at around 1,400m (4,600ft), are not as high as
those of the Dikti Range but this does not always make for gentler
contours and there are many spectacular views and rock formations
visible in this region.

## The North Coast

There is a good road from Ayios Nikolaos to Sitia which, when it
climbs into the mountains beyond Pachia Amnos, offers some of the
most magnificent views on the whole island. It is, however, a fairly
long drive (70km, 43 miles).

Heading east out of Ayios Nikolaos, there are numerous beaches,
all close to the road and of similar quality, although those near the
town can be crowded. Most have some watersports facilities and are
shallow with sandy beaches.

The first village of any size is **Istro**, 9.5km (6 miles) from Ayios
Nikolaos, once known as *Vrokastro*. It is set back on the road and
looks down to the coast. There are shops, a petrol station and several
tracks leading to the shore. The best beach seems to be the one on the
way out of the village, heading east. Look for cars parked just off the

road and a short path down to the sandy cove with its incredibly clear, turquoise water. The bay is sheltered and ideal for swimming or waterskiing. At Istro is the first of the roads which cross the island to the south coast and which are described later in this chapter.

From Istro, the cliffs become steeper and access to the shore more difficult until the Gournia Moon campsite and Pachia Amnos just beyond it. Before these is a track off to the right to the Faneromeni Convent, reached after 5km (3 miles) of difficult driving on a dirt road. The buildings are not that old and include a church which was built over a hermit's grotto. The views at the top are rewarding as the convent is perched high in the cliffs. (This convent should not be confused with that of the same name near Sitia).

Just beyond the track to Faneromeni, on the right, is *Gournia*. This is 19km (12 miles) from Ayios Nikolaos and is an important Minoan site. It was excavated early this century and revealed a working town with the remains of workshops for pottery, carpentry and metalwork. It was clearly a crowded place to live, with small houses of several storeys packed closely together. The streets are easily discernible but the small palace, theatral area and central court are harder to identify, the latter is uphill at the top of the site. A shrine was found; about 100m (330ft) straight ahead from the modern entrance and then slightly to the right. This contained a large number of clay figurines and religious vessels to add to the numerous working implements ranging from saws to tweezers.

The site covers an area of 15,000m² (49,000ft²) and clearly its position so close to the sea must have made the town strategically important. Whether it was independent or linked to the Minoan palaces is unknown and there are no references to the city in myths or Classical works of literature. It seems to have followed the pattern of these palaces with the first settlement in the Early Minoan period which continued to expand until 1450BC, the year of the catastrophe which destroyed this and all the other Minoan sites.

*Gournia* makes a refreshing change from the other, more popular, sites and adds to the insights gained from the palaces by showing a different sort of Minoan life; the practical rather than the artistic. The best views of the layout of the town are looking back from the road as it begins to climb although it is difficult for drivers to find anywhere safe to stop.

**Pachia Amnos** (Pahia Ammos) is a village by a long, sandy beach with a few tavernas and rooms available. Unfortunately, large

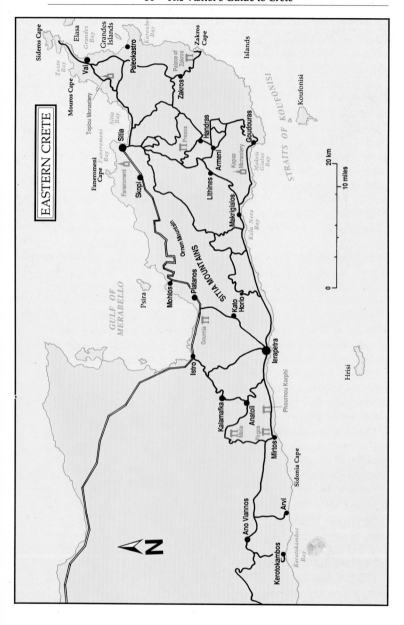

*The important Minoan site at* Gournia

amounts of rubbish tend to be washed up on the shore in this region and it is therefore not a very pleasant place to swim. It also marks the start of the plastic greenhouses in which bananas are grown. The second road across to the south coast leaves from here and this is the narrowest part of the island.

The route along the coast begins its most spectacular section with the road lined, in the summer months, by the pink and white flowers of the oleander, enhancing the stunning views down over the sea.

**Kavousi** is the first mountain village reached as the road begins to climb steeply and is particularly pretty with its flowery gardens. Above Kavousi are several minor Minoan sites and several pleasant, if steep, walks up to these and into the hills beyond.

A few kilometres further on is **Platanos**, not big enough to be marked on most maps but a recognised viewing point with places to park and look out over the Gulf of Merabello and Psira Island.

Psira was inhabited by the Minoans and seems to have been a flourishing trading port. Numerous houses have been uncovered over a wide area and a fresco was found in one of the larger houses, along with substantial finds of finely decorated pottery. There is also evidence of Roman occupation of the island, perhaps as a military outpost. Today it is a sanctuary for the kri-kri wild goat and boat trips are organised from Ayios Nikolaos.

**Mohlos** is one of the few parts of the coast accessible in this region and even here it is far from easy to get to the sea. The village is only reached after at least 5km (3miles) of driving on dirt roads. There are numerous different tracks whose surfaces are all equally bad. However, there is a surprising amount of development in Mohlos, including several tavernas and even a hotel.

Offshore is an island, also called Mohlos, which was settled in Minoan times when it was probably joined to the mainland. Several important tombs, called house tombs because of their numerous different rooms, were found here and the richness of the jewellery inside them indicates they belonged to an affluent family. There are also remains of a Byzantine and Roman settlement and fortifications from this period can be seen on the far side of the island.

The main road continues through several pleasant mountain villages; with others like **Mirsini** just off the road and often worth a detour to stop at a café or to see one of the numerous Byzantine churches of the region. These are usually locked and finding someone with a key may be difficult.

The Mouliana region, which includes the villages of **Exo Mouliana** and **Mesa Mouliana**, is known for its wine and sultanas which are harvested towards the end of the summer when there is a sultana festival in Sitia.

Skopi is a large village of little interest but down a road to the right is the village of **Khameizi** (Chamezi) with a Minoan site of some importance because the house uncovered there was a unique oval shape. The site is not easy to find and even the archaeologist who discovered the site points out that it is, 'not easily accessible'. Those wishing to visit it should ask for instructions in the village. In the village itself, there is a small folklore museum.

Beyond Skopi there is a track down to the Faneromeni Monastery, a rough drive but worthwhile for the views of the sea. The monastery itself was destroyed in a fire, leaving only a precariously placed chapel (built over a cave) amidst the blackened ruins. This grotto is still an important shrine today and much visited by pilgrims.

The final approaches to Sitia are not especially interesting as the landscape flattens out and the sea disappears from view.

## Places of Interest Between Ayios Nikolaos and Sitia

**Istro**
A small holiday village with several good beaches in the coves beyond it.

**Mohlos**
A village and offshore island with extensive Minoan remains.

**Gournia**
An important and densely populated Minoan town, revealing the industriousness of its residents with potteries,

carpentries and other workshops that have been discovered.

**Platanos**
The best viewing point to see the Gulf of Merabello and the islands from the road high up above the shore.

**Sitia**
A large port town with a restored Venetian fortress and an archaeological museum. It is famous for its sultanas.

Sitia is the fifth biggest town on the island but, with a population of only 8,000, it cannot claim to be a sizeable place. Much of its importance comes from its port which is deep enough to take large cruise ships or tankers. A weekly ferry service to Rhodes also calls here. An airport opened near the town in 1984 but so far only operates an occasional flight to Rhodes.

The early origins of the town are blurred and open to archaeological argument. It was probably inhabited by the Minoans and was the city of *Eteia* during the Classical Greek period. There was a brief Byzantine occupation and the Genoese had a foothold here but, as ever, it was the Venetians who brought prosperity and constructed the fortifications around the town. Several disastrous earthquakes, along with pirate raids by Barbarossa, caused considerable damage and although it held out against the Turks for three years, they eventually destroyed the whole city. It was left unoccupied for 200 years and only rebuilt towards the end of Turkish occupation. As a result, the town is distinctly modern and very little evidence of its history is visible.

One of its few claims to fame is that Vincentzos Kornaros, who wrote the epic poem *Erotokritos*, was born here or in a nearby village.

Indeed, Kornaros remains a common name in the region. The poem is a long account of ill-starred love which finally triumphs. Despite its rather obscure style, it is popular with peasants who know it by heart — the poem and author are much revered. Performances are sometimes given during the cultural festival which is held in Iraklion every summer.

The town is not usually busy and parking is easy along the seafront where there is a cabin which claims to be the tourist office but is rarely open. There are a few hotels but it is not a major tourist centre. Those tourists who do come tend to be Italian or French, the former perhaps because the Italians occupied the town during World War II. The tavernas are strung along the harbour which is a rather large expanse of concrete, enlivened only by the resident pelican.

*Pelican at Sitia*

The restored Venetian fortress is now used as an open-air theatre and is worth visiting. It lies at the end of Arkhadious Street which also contains the Folklore Museum. This building houses a collection of local crafts, especially weaving. Archaeologists claim to have uncovered Roman fish tanks further along the waterfront but as these are partially submerged, they are not easy to find.

On the Sitia to Ierapetra road is the Archaeological Museum

*Toplou Monastery*

which contains finds from the local area. The first exhibit is a case of pottery and stone axes from the Neolithic period that were found in a cave near *Zakros*. Several cases are devoted to finds from the cemetery at **Ayia Photia**, 5km (3 miles) east of Sitia. The Minoan tombs on this site revealed a very rich collection of artefacts. A large number of clay figurines from peak sanctuaries are displayed in subsequent cases.

The islands of Mohlos and Psira supplied a whole range of exhibits, especially jars and vases. Finds from the town at Paleokastro fill a whole case and include cups and vases. The most impressive artefacts come from the palace at *Zakros* and include a wine press blackened in the fire which followed the catastrophe of 1450BC and a tablet bearing Linear A script. The collection is completed with finds from the Graeco-Roman period, some found in Sitia itself during roadworks. At the end of August the town hosts the annual sultana festival; a celebration of the harvest of the crop for which the region is famous.

From Sitia, visitors can either cross to the south of the island (a region which will be described later) or continue out to the far east.

## The Far East

Just outside Sitia is **Ayia Photia** (Aghia Fotia), a village where the largest Minoan cemetery in Crete has been found. It contained more than 250 tombs and finds included 1,500 vases; the largest Minoan dagger ever discovered; various other weapons and Minoan fish hooks. Most of these objects are now in Iraklion Museum.

There are several sites of interest on the Itanos Peninsula, all are well-signposted and on good roads. The first of these is the Toplou Monastery which is 16km (12miles) from Sitia. The monastery's most striking aspect is its strong defensive fortifications which are a testament to the frequent attacks it has suffered from pirates and invading forces. The word *toplou* is Turkish for cannon. In fact, it has always been a centre of resistance to occupying powers, most recently against the Germans, and this resistance has always resulted in severe reprisals.

The monastery was founded in the fourteenth century but the building was destroyed in an earthquake in 1612, after which it was rebuilt in its current form. It has always been a very wealthy establishment and still owns much of the land in the region. There are only three monks left today and they seem to keep out of the way, apart from one who checks visitors' dress — no shorts or bare shoulders are permitted.

The church is in a small courtyard around which are the arched entrances to the cells. It is famous for its icons, some of which are very rare. The best-known is *Lord Thou art Great*, by Ioannis Kornaros. This depicts sixty-one scenes from the Orthodox liturgy; there are a profusion of figures and animals, both naturalistic and imaginary, along with many well-known biblical figures. Postcards of the icon are available to allow greater study of the detail, and there is a small café just outside the monastery selling drinks and ice creams.

**Vai Beach**, 25km (15$^1/_2$ miles) from Sitia, is perhaps the most visited place in the region. Its attraction is what the postcards describe as 'the only self-propagated palm grove in Europe'. Further exoticism is added by the story that the palms grew from date stones left by Phoenecian traders.

The palms do make an impressive contrast to the stumpy olive trees more usual in the region and there are a large number of them both at Vai itself and on the approaches to it. The beach is sandy and pleasant but it is only the backdrop of palm trees which distinguish it from many others. The fundamental drawback of Vai is that by midday, large numbers of coaches draw up in the purpose-built car park, which even has the luxury of public toilets, and the beach becomes unbearably crowded.

One option is to retreat up the road to **Itanos**; a smaller beach with only one palm tree and the ruins of an important Classical town which was also inhabited by the Romans. Even this beach may become crowded at the height of the season and further searching of the coast may be necessary to find peace and quiet.

**Paleokastro** (Palekastro) is the largest settlement in the area, with a modern church in its central square, several rooms to rent and a few restaurants. It is a couple of kilometres from the sea and there are reasonable beaches down a dusty track from the centre of the village.

There are also the remains of a Minoan town on the way to the beach. It seems to have been a sizeable place, dating from the Late Minoan period with streets and houses uncovered. Further excavations are planned to try and uncover the extent of the site but currently there is very little to see other than overgrown walls and piles of stones.

The main destination south of Paleokastro is the palace at *Zakros,*

## Places of Interest in The Far East

**Toplou Monastery**
Famous for its *Lord Thou art Great* icon, this is a fortified monastery in an isolated setting.

**Itanos**
Alternative beach to Vai and the site of a Classical Greek town.

**Vai Beach**
A beach lined with palm trees making an exotic if sometimes crowded location.

**Paleokastro**
A useful stopping off point; a sizeable village with cafés round the main square. Close by are a beach and the site of a Minoan town.

**Palace of Zakros**
The smallest of the Minoan palaces, only discovered in 1962. It is unusual for being so close to the sea and for being unplundered when discovered.

26km (16 miles) away on a reasonable road which passes through low hills and some small villages.

Ano Zakros is not a particularly interesting village. It was once known for its springs but nowadays very few people stay here, preferring to continue straight on to the Minoan palace 8km (5 miles) away in the village at Kato Zakros. Just outside Ano Zakros is a sign to a Minoan villa where a wine press and several giant pithoi storage jars were found.

The drive down to the coast is an impressive one with fine views of the sea below. On the final approach to the village, caves can be seen in the cliffs beyond. These were Minoan tombs and gave the name to the 'Valley of the Dead' Ravine which descends beside them.

**Kato Zakros** is a very quiet place with only a few tavernas, a deserted pebbly beach and no other facilities. The palace is at the far end of the village, about 100m (330ft) inland. This was once a paved road leading to the harbour installations which are now no longer visible. It is the smallest Minoan palace and distinctive for being built so close to the sea and not having a separate port. Excavations only began in earnest in 1961 and generated much excitement as few had expected to discover a totally new site of this extent. For some unknown reason, it had not been plundered and so yielded very rich finds of jewellery. Excavations still continue, working to uncover the town on the hill behind the site.

*The 'Valley of the Dead', Zakros*

The palace follows the usual pattern of Minoan construction, built in 1900BC, probably on the site of a Neolithic settlement, destroyed in 1700BC and then rebuilt. It is believed to have played a significant role in trade with Egypt, but its relationship with *Knossos* is unclear. It suffered the same catastrophe as the other palaces in 1450BC and it was not resettled or reoccupied after this. Volcanic rock found here is used as evidence by those who believe this disaster was caused by an eruption on the island of Santorini (Thera). This is is not conclusive proof because volcanic pumice had many uses and could have been imported here rather than deposited in the aftermath of an eruption.

Finding such an important site was something of a surprise as early excavations had led to a belief that this was simply a minor settlement. It has served as an inspiration to those who believe more Minoan palaces lie buried around the island.

The modern entrance leads into an internal courtyard which has a bath in one corner, and then passes through into the central court which measures 30.3m by 12.15m (99ft by 40ft). The west wing contains the hall of ceremonies where it is thought religious rites were performed and leads into a room which is believed to have been a banqueting hall. A Lustral basin is also visible in this part of the palace, along with a treasury which yielded many stone vases, axes and ivory artefacts.

The south wing seems to have contained workshops while the east wing housed the royal apartments which have been extensively damaged by ploughing before the site was discovered. The circular cistern is the most striking object in the palace and still contains water. According to one unlikely suggestion, it was a Minoan swimming pool. A sunken spring and a circular well seem to have been the water sources for the palace and provide further evidence for the sophistication of Minoan drainage systems. The town is on the hill behind the site and, as it is still being excavated, is not open to the public.

There is a track south of Ano Zakros which leads to **Xerokambos**, a beautiful isolated beach which still manages to have a taverna but the road is unpaved all the way. From Xerokambos it is possible to cut across to Ziro but the track is appalling and it is more sensible and quicker to return to Sitia and cross the island on the tarred road.

## Routes Across the Island

There are three roads which cross the island in this eastern region, the shortest being that from Pachia Amnos where the island is only 14km ($8^1/_2$ miles) wide although the bends in the road extend this distance to 35km (22miles) for the motorist.

The road from Istro is a slow one as it passes through the mountains. Just outside Istro is Kalo Khorio and there is a wide assortment of ruins on top of the steep hill behind the village. These date mainly from the early Post Minoan period, around 1200BC, and are typical of the smaller sites. It includes a few houses tightly packed together and arranged in terraces and a few tombs.

**Kalamafka**, perched high up on the rocks, is the only other place on the road worth a stop. It offers the unique possibility of views of both north and south coasts.

At Anatoli it is possible to make a detour further into the mountains through several little villages. The road ends at *Malla*, the site of a Classical Greek city state; no excavations have taken place so the site is of little interest. Otherwise the road descends to the coast just west of Ierapetra.

# Places of Interest on The South Coast

**Kapsa Monastery**
A somewhat out-of-the-way place, perched on a cliff; the monastery contains the body of the eccentric monk Gerontyiannis, a local folk hero.

**Goudhouras**
The furthest beach beyond the monastery, isolated but still manages to have some tourist development.

**Analipsi/Makrigialos**
Dusty coastal resorts with a splendid, long beach, shallow sea and sandy shore.

**Ierapetra**
A busy coastal town with several crumbling ruins including a mosque and a Venetian fortress. The fruit market has much local colour.

**Mirtos**
A pretty village with a good beach and two Minoan sites in the hills behind.

**Arvi**
A beach after a long, winding drive down a steep mountain road. This is supposedly the centre of a sub-tropical microclimate.

**Kerotakambos**
Another isolated beach some distance down the steep mountain side from the main road.

The second route across the island leaves from Pachia Amnos and has mountains dominating the views to the east, with the impressive Monastaraki Gorge clearly visible.

Three kilometres (2miles) along the road is a right turn to **Vasiliki**, a very old site dating from the earliest Minoan period around 2500BC. There is a small palace, along with several other later houses. The most important finds were of Vasiliki ware, very old pottery with a distinctive red and brown colouring in a blotchy pattern which is thought to have first been created by accident and then later used as a deliberate design. There is evidence of a settlement here right up to the Roman period but it is the fact that the site is so old that is of the main interest for archaeologists.

**Episkopi** is the mid-point of the route and has an old medieval church with unusual decoration. From here the road descends quickly into the centre of Ierapetra.

The final possibility is to cross the island from Sitia which is a much longer trip (64km, 40 miles) and the scenery is not as impressive on this drive.

*Ahladia*, off right from the road, and *Zou*, to the left, are minor Minoan sites of interest only to the enthusiast, although the Minoan house at *Zou* is well-preserved and there are good views of the surrounding area. About half way across the island is the much more important site of *Praesos* (*Presos*) which was a city state in Classical Greek times and was first excavated late last century. It is important because it was inhabited by the Eteocretans, the descendants of the Minoans, and it is the survival of the Minoan influence which is of most interest. Unfortunately, the importance of the site is not reflected in the remains visible to the visitor.

The road continues further into the mountains with more minor sites at Handras, Armeni and Ziros. It is a pleasant drive and just before Handras there is a ruined village called Voila which was abandoned in the seventeenth century. There are also Venetian remains in the area including a villa at *Eteia* (*Etia*).

**Lithines** is the next village of any size on the main road which descends quickly from here down to the coast. On the way there are several signs to the Kapsa Monastery; the best turning is that which runs along the coast, being both the easiest drive and offering the opportunity to stop at beaches on the way.

The monastery is 10km (6 miles) away on an unpaved road and is sited high up on the cliffs. It was founded by the Venetians but only came to prominence in the nineteenth century and most of its buildings originate from this period.

It contains the body of an eccentric monk, Gerontoyiannis, who had a reputation for helping the poor and performing miracles, feats which gave him the status of a saint amongst the locals. There are several beaches beyond the monastery and, at Goudouras, a collection of tavernas before the track turns back inland.

**Analipsi** and **Makrigialos** are two villages which run into each other where the Sitia road meets the coast. They consist of new building on either side of the street. They have plenty of rooms to rent and a very good, long and sandy beach.

Beyond Makrigialos there are very few accessible parts of the coast. There are a few reasonable beaches in the region but they are not really worth the perilous descent required to reach them, especially as these small strips of sand tend to get crowded very quickly. Apart from a couple of campsites, there is very little in the way of

*Ierapetra*

tourist development between here and Ierapetra.

**Ierapetra** is the fourth largest city on the island, with a population of 10,750. There is a reasonable amount of accommodation available in rooms and there are numerous hotels to cope with the surprising number of package tourists who come here. Restaurants are plentiful and are concentrated along the sea front beyond the harbour. All other facilities; post office, phone office and banks, are within easy walking distance of the shore. The tourist office is next to the police station, between a pleasant shady little park and the beach. They are particularly friendly and are willing to give information.

There is evidence of Minoan occupation on the site and it became an important city state, *Hieraptyna*, in Classical times, known for its constant wars with its neighbours. It strongly resisted Roman invasion but, after surrendering, became an important port for the invaders when its proximity to Egypt made it a vital gateway to Africa.

The town seems to have flourished during the Byzantine period and was then occupied by the Venetians who built the fort which was destroyed by an earthquake and had to be rebuilt. The Turks took over in 1647 and left their usual legacy of mosques. Frequent earthquakes have obliterated most of the city's historical remains leaving only a few later remnants.

The Venetian Fortress is in the west of the town beyond the beach and dates from the thirteenth century. Claims that it has been restored seem to be somewhat exaggerated and at the time of writing there are no signs of it being open to the public.

Opposite the fort is a pretty, twin-domed church and, through a maze of narrow alleys, is the mosque which retains its minaret but is falling to bits. The city's claim to fame is that Napoleon slept here on his way to Egypt and a house near the seafront proudly proclaims this fact; several of the restaurants have seized on this motif for their names.

The Archaeological Museum, which has recently reopened, houses local finds of no great importance. The most significant exhibit is a Minoan sarcophagus found in Episkopi and decorated with intricate depictions of everyday scenes. The rest of the collection consists of statues and a few coins from the Roman period.

One of the most rewarding places to visit in Ierapetra is the fruit market on Adr Kostoua which has a wonderful atmosphere and cheap fruit.

There is a long beach in the town itself and the possibility of an excursion to **Gaidouronisi**, or Donkey Island, which is 13km (8 miles) away. It is uninhabited and boasts fine, sandy beaches and clear water; there is a boat from Ierapetra every day.

Overall, it is a busy little town, perhaps not ideal for a long stay but definitely worth a visit.

## West of Ierapetra to Ano Viannos

There is little of interest on the main coast road out of Ierapetra until **Nea Mirtos**, 17km (10$^1$/$_2$ miles) from Ierapetra, where there are two archaeological sites and a pleasant beach. The first site is a couple of kilometres before Nea Mirtos and is known as *Phornou Korphi* (*Fournoukorifi*) — it is best approached on foot up the hill. It is still difficult to find and there is not much to see when you arrive, again it is important simply by virtue of being so old. It was an early Minoan settlement dating from 2660BC where pottery and a large number of clay figurines were found in a shrine.

The second site, known as *Pirgos*, is on the eastern side of the river-bed on a hill, again accessible only on foot. There was a two- or three-storey Minoan villa from about 1600BC on the site and a town around it. A fire in the 1450BC catastrophe seems to have caused major damage and volcanic pumice rock found here lends support to the theory of the volanic eruption on Santorini causing that destruction.

A left turn off the main road leads to the village of **Mirtos**; a quiet place to stop with numerous tavernas spread out along the shore and a long, fine beach which continues west for some distance.

After Mirtos, the road begins to climb into the mountains with some rapidity, passing through several villages but it is generally a very quiet stretch of easy driving. At Amiras there is a turning down to Arvi which is 14km (8$^1$/$_2$ miles) away; either go through the village itself taking the left fork at the far end, or continue along the main road and turn at the huge war memorial which dominates the hill. This route enters the village at the western end and the turning is then a sharp right. The road down the mountainside is narrow and steep; although it is tarmac all the way, it is a difficult drive with very tight bends on the final approaches to the village.

The area is reputed to be a micro-climate with tropical temperatures allowing the cultivation of pineapples and other exotic fruit. **Arvi** itself has a few tavernas and shops but can be something of a

*Roadside shrine, Arvi*

*A colourful corner of Arvi*

disappointment, bearing in mind the difficulty in getting there. The beach is long but pebbly and can be dirty.

The main road continues through the mountains to **Ano Viannos**, a big village high in the mountains with two Byzantine churches and a much larger modern one on the main road. It is also the legendary site of a battle between two Gods; the giant twins, Otas and Ephiates.

Just beyond the village is a road down to Keratokambos, 10km (6miles) of difficult driving with only part of the road paved. It passes through **Hondros**, a pretty little village, and then to the coast, where there is a very quiet beach with the usual few cafés and the odd room here or in the villages on the approaches.

It is possible to continue across the island to the Messara Plain on the main road but there is a fairly long, unpaved section between Demati and Ano Kasteliana which is passable but very slow. However, all detours to avoid this stretch are equally time consuming, with the twisting mountain roads making for a long trip either way. This part of the island is described in the South of Iraklion chapter.

# 2
# *IRAKLION TO*
# *AYIOS NIKOLAOS*

---

This stretch of coastline is the most visited part of Crete, with Malia, Hersonissos and Ayios Nikolaos being the destination of most package tourists from Britain. However, this influx has not spoiled the region and it is still relatively easy to escape off the beaten track and discover both the picturesque and the unexpected.

## Iraklion to Malia

There are two roads which lead east out of Iraklion, the old and the new. The new one is a fast, uninteresting highway which offers few opportunities to explore the surrounding countryside. However, for those wishing to cover the 65km (40 miles) to Ayios Nikolaos, this is clearly the best route and the trip can easily be made in 45 minutes.

The old road follows the coast closely until it joins the new road at Kato Gouves and offers a much more interesting drive, not least for the views of the planes coming in to land at Iraklion airport.

This stretch of coastline has several reasonable beaches which are sandy and wide enough for sunbathers to get away from the traffic. The resorts around these beaches are less attractive. They tend to be built close to the road which, although superseded by the new highway, is still busy.

Beyond **Amnissos**, where there is a beach and a historical site (see Iraklion chapter), is a detour inland which passes under the main highway to the Eileithyia Cave. There was a shrine to Eileithyia, the goddess of fertility, and many remains of offerings were found here.

These dated mainly from the Post Minoan period although it is clear that certain aspects of Minoan religion were absorbed into the culture of those that succeeded it. The cave was even mentioned by Homer, Odysseus having been blown off course and forced to anchor at 'Amnisus, by the cave of Eileithyia'. These days, the cave is fenced off and closed to the public although special permission to visit may be gained through the tourist office.

**Kokkino Hani** (Kokkini Hani) claims to be a holiday resort but contains only a few shops and restaurants strung along the road and has no distinctive character whatsoever. A short distance to the east is *Nirou Hani (Nirou Megaron)*; a Minoan villa excavated at the beginning of this century. Its main interest lies in the number of objects associated with religious rituals that were found. These include an enormous bronze double axe, now in Iraklion Museum, forty altars and various lamps. One theory is that this villa served as a central storage point from where missionaries set out to bring Minoan religion to the heathens. Although this seems a little fantastic, no other, more realistic theories have been suggested. The site is open to the public, although inside parts are fenced off.

There is an American base at Gournes and photography is forbidden inside the military zone. Gouves is a village lying to the south of the road and just beyond it is the Skotino Cave, whose entrance is marked by the Venetian church of Ayia Paraskevi. The cave is one of the deepest on the island and is one of the most impressive. The largest cavern is 90m (295ft) long and 12m (39ft) high. Finds ranging from the Neolithic to Roman periods have been discovered and, like so many others, the cave clearly had some kind of religious importance. Indeed, some claim that this was the labyrinth in which the Minotaur was kept.

**Kato Gouves** is at the junction of the old and new roads and is a small village with a reasonable beach. This is quite hard to find; follow the signs to the Astir Hotel. By the sea, there is a tarmac road which runs along the shore back towards the military base. The beach is narrow and therefore the road often seems too close for comfort. The resort itself has a strange atmosphere, lacking any real centre and consisting simply of a few shops and hotels with dusty scrubland in between.

There are several other beaches in the area where the mountain route from Kastelli reaches the coast. Some of these are quite good and usually quiet; simply follow the signs put up by the proprietors of the seaside tavernas. The Kastelli road is one of the routes up to the Lasithi Plateau which is described later.

It is now that the major resorts are encountered and it becomes more difficult for the independent traveller to find somewhere to stay. **Limin Hersonissos** (Limin Hersonisou) is permanently busy, with all the usual souvenir shops along the main road, along with the additional and very real hazard of holidaymakers on mopeds. The beach is narrow and although it is sandy, it is interrupted by several rocky outcrops and is invariably crowded.

The Romans were the first invaders of Hersonissos. They built the harbour and fortified the church of Ayia Paraskevi. On the seaward side of the harbour wall are several rectangular shapes cut out of the rock which are believed to be Roman fish tanks. It was also an important Byzantine centre and the remains of fifth-century churches have been found nearby. Today, there is a solid line of tavernas fronting the sea with a range of modern souvenir shops.

**Stalis**, or Stalidas, is a resort which is much smaller than Herssonisos or Malia but has potential to rival them if development continues. Its roads are still dirt tracks and getting in and out involves making dangerous turns off the main road. It consists of a few hotels, apartments and restaurants near the beach which is reasonable and not too crowded.

**Malia** is the next resort along the road, a few kilometres beyond another turning to the Lasithi Plateau. It has a long, sandy beach and an offshore islet. The town can be divided into three areas; despite the number of tourists, it is not really a very big place. The first area is inland behind the main road; this is the old town, consisting of a maze of narrow alleys which are a nightmare for drivers. There are a few restaurants and rooms to rent but most of the pandemonium in this part of the town is caused by the locals blocking the road rather than tourists.

The main Ayios Nikolaos road constitutes the second part of town along which there are various shops, cafés and supermarkets. At the western end of this road, the beach is signposted and the street leading down to the shore constitutes the third and most tourist-oriented area. This road is lined with cafés, discos and restaurants, all clearly designed to entertain British tourists. Of further interest are the enormous souvenir shops; one has three floors, which are open until late at night.

Those seeking culture should head to the east of the town. Down

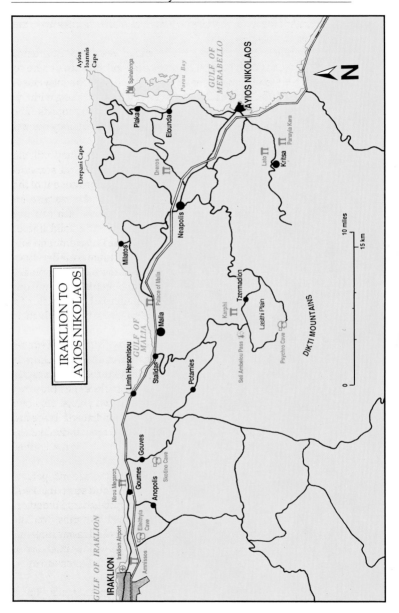

π a track just off the main road is the Palace of Malia. This is one of the great Minoan sites along with *Knossos* and *Phaestos*. However, its low walls, combined with the fact that some of the site is still being excavated, mean that it is not as impressive as either of the other two.

Some Neolithic remains have been found but the Old Palace dates from 1900BC. It was destroyed in 1700BC and rebuilt but, in 1450BC, it suffered in whatever catastrophe it was that hit Crete and caused the destruction of all the Minoan palaces. It is thought this palace belonged to Sarpedon, Minos' youngest brother, just as *Phaestos* belonged to the middle brother Radamanthys.

The palace is slightly smaller than *Phaestos* but has a similar design, being built around a central court. The entrance is through the west court; further south are eight storage pits which were presumably granaries. You quickly come to the focus of the building; the central court. On the western side of the court is the famous Malia Kernos; a round slab with a hole in the middle and thirty-four smaller, circular indentations around the circumference. Numerous uses have been claimed for this, the most likely being that it contained different offerings for use in rituals. A rather more unlikely suggestion is that it was a Minoan roulette wheel.

The central court measures 48m by 22m (157ft by 72ft) with an altar in the middle. At the far end are a series of storerooms while to the west are a number of rooms connected with religious rituals. These include a room raised from the court, called the Loggia by archaeologists; this is presumed to be where the religious ceremonies took place while the crowd observed from the central court.

The entrance to the north wing was built around a series of pillars, the bases of which remain today. From here you enter a large hall which could have been a dining room. The royal apartments were at the western end of the north wing.

The palace is only one part of the whole site, the rest of which is gradually being uncovered to reveal a town of some size with several large houses. A royal tomb was discovered near the shore. This was called Khrysolakos, translated as the 'Gold Pit', where some very fine Minoan gold jewellery was uncovered, including the Bee Pendant, now in Iraklion Museum. The tomb contained several different burial chambers and probably belonged to the members of the same royal family.

## Places of Interest from Iraklion to Malia

**Amnissos**
A beach and the site of a Minoan villa, perhaps the harbour for *Knossos*.

**Limin Nirou**
Site of a curious Minoan store-house for a whole range of religious objects. Close to the beach.

**Kato Gouves**
A village with a few hotels and a reasonable beach that is a little difficult to find.

**Hersonissos**
The first of the big resorts, it claims to have twenty-one discos along with all the other tourist facilities and some history in the form of a Roman harbour.

**Malia**
Another resort popular with those on package holidays, it has a reasonable beach which is usually very crowded. The little alleys behind the town are more interesting than the cafés and discos on the approach to the beach.

**Palace at Malia**
The third of the great Minoan palaces built close to the sea on distinctive orange rock. The palace is not reconstructed and all that is visible are low walls from which the layout can be determined.

## The Lasithi Plateau

There are three possible routes up to this much-visited plateau, best known for its windmills. Some claim there are over 10,000 of these on the plain but keen eyesight and a good imagination will be required to spot even half this number as many are derelict. Their primary purpose of pumping water has been rendered inefficient by modern machinery.

It is, however, the landscape which is the most impressive sight. The extensive plain is at a height of 850m, (2,788ft). The fertility of the land is clearly evident from its green and yellow pattern of fields, stretching out to the slopes of the mountains which enclose it.

The first possible route to Lasithi heads inland on the Kastelli road and then bears left towards Potamies, where there is a Byzantine church with restored frescoes and the church of a tenth century-monastery, Panayia Gouverniotisa. From here the road climbs gently until it joins the second route to the plateau.

This second route leaves the coast at Stalis and is by far the more spectacular. The road climbs steeply in long bends above the coast and offers incredible views back towards the resorts and the coastline beyond them.

This road is signposted **Mohos** which is about 9km ($5^1/_2$ miles) from the turning. It is an attractive village with a church at its centre and cafés grouped around the square, making it a pleasant place to break the journey.

The route continues to climb beyond Mohos but less steeply for a while until joined by the other inland road. To the left is a detour to **Krasi**, a village which claims to have the oldest plane tree in Europe. This certainly is enormous and casts shadows in the late afternoon over the taverna in the centre of the village. It reputedly takes twelve local men to fully enclose it with their arms. Opposite, on the other side of the road are a number of mountain springs, spoiled by the amount of rubbish thrown into them.

Also in Krasi is the energetically advertised 200-year-old Cretan house. It is, in fact, a souvenir shop and the proprietor gives 20 second 'tours', pointing out the oven and the grape press and then waits expectantly for a purchase to be made.

To the right of the road, at **Kera**, is the Kardiotissa Convent with frescoes dating from the fourteenth century which were discovered underneath more modern works. It also offers good views of the surrounding countryside.

Beyond Kera, the road begins to climb steeply again and then, quite suddenly, arrives at the Seli Ambelou Pass at a height of 900m (2,952ft) with the plain spread out below. There is a line of derelict windmills on the hillside which look like curious insects. They are actually souvenir shops, but it is still one of the most impressive viewpoints on the island.

With only a few passes through the mountains onto the plateau, it can often be cut off by snow in winter. Its geography also makes it easy to defend and it was a major centre of resistance against the Venetians who eventually forcibly removed the population from the plain in an attempt to subdue them.

The rich soil makes the area exceptionally fertile and crops, including apples, potatoes and wheat, are grown here. The plateau is also known for its wild flowers, especially its orchids. There are twenty-one villages which are sited round the edge of the plain to avoid flooding and it is the only upland plain on the island that is inhabited all the year round.

The other route to the plateau comes in from the east, setting off from Neapolis and leading through several pretty mountain villages and over a number of high mountain passes with the road climbing steeply from Zernia.

The best way to see the plateau is to follow the road which encircles it and which passes through all the villages. **Tzermadion** (Tzermiadon) is the biggest village, although its population is barely over 1,000. There are places to stay here, a post office and numerous shops. The area is known for its weaving which is hung from virtually every shop on the main street, clearly catering for the large number of coach parties that come on organised visits.

There is a cave near the village known either as the Trapeza Cave or the Kronos Cave. It is erratically signposted and requires a 10 minute walk from the main road which runs behind Tzermadion. Neolithic remains were found in the cave along with 100 bodies, marking it out as a burial site. It is, however, neither as important nor as impressive as the Diktean Cave on the other side of the plateau.

*Karphi* is an important site above Tzermadion, accessible only on foot and involving a steep climb of about 1 hour. It was excavated by the famous British archaeologist John Pendlebury, who was later killed during the Battle of Crete. It was a Minoan Peak sanctuary; a place of worship around which a settlement was built which included a temple. It was later inhabited by the last of the Minoans who were probably fleeing the Mycenean invaders and seeking refuge in the mountains. The site is important archaeologically but there is very little for the amateur to see.

**Ayios Constandinos** (Aghios Konstantinos) is another tourist-oriented village which lies close to the junction where the road from Neapolis arrives at the plateau. A couple of kilometres further is Ayios Yeorgios (Aghios Georgios) which is a much quieter place. There is a folklore museum which is well-signposted and closes at 4pm. It contains, among other exhibits, stuffed birds and human models.

There are several other smaller hamlets before **Psychro** (Psihro) which is the most famous of the Lasithi villages. Just beyond the village is the Psychro Cave (also known as the Dikteian Cave), one of several legendary birthplaces claimed for Zeus.

The road leads up to a large car park from where there are good views across the plateau. It is here that the visitor will be approached by guides who attempt to frighten you into accepting their services with tales of the enormous depth of the cavern; anything from 100m to 250m (330ft to 820ft), in reality it is 65m (213ft). They will also warn of its slipperiness and its darkness. While the latter may be true, the single, flickering candle of a guide is of little help. Sensible shoes and a decent torch make a guide unnecessary, unless a little local flavour is desired.

The entrance to the cave is a good 15 minute walk up a stony path and lies at a height of 1,025m (3,362ft). Mules are available for those who prefer to rely on the legs of others.

Legend has it that Rhea gave birth to Zeus in the cave because Kronos, his father, fearing a son would usurp him, resolved to eat all his offspring. However, this time Rhea tricked him by giving him a stone to swallow and left Zeus here where he was nurtured by various wild animals and protected by warriors called Curetes who danced and banged their shields to drown the sound of the baby's crying. The cave revealed numerous religious offerings, covering the range of cultures from Minoan to Roman. Another alleged inhabitant was Epimenides, the Classical poet and mystic, who spent many years of contemplation in the cave.

The cave is undeniably dramatic, having been left, apart from a wooden handrail, in a totally natural state. Of course there is not that much to see, although guides will point out all kinds of weird and wonderful rocks, including those representing the nipples at which Zeus is supposed to have fed. Overall, it is simply an interesting experience to splash about at the bottom of the cave and take in the atmosphere.

Between Psychro and the various routes back there are few villages, simply the ever present spectacle of the plain itself.

## Malia to Ayios Nikolaos

The main new road turns inland soon after Malia and quickly crosses to Ayios Nikolaos, the drive offers the rare chance to pass through a tunnel.

There are numerous places worth visiting off the main roads in this region. The first of these is **Sisi**, just off the old Ayios Nikolaos road; a beach resort with a quiet harbour although the amount of building going on suggests it is unlikely to remain quiet for long.

**Milatos**, beyond Sisi on a narrow road, is without tourism, being a very old village with a maze of streets, one of which leads to the beach some 2km (1 mile) away. Here there is more development but even this only amounts to a few tavernas. The village is known for its

# Places of Interest on the Lasithi Plateau

**Mohos**
A pretty mountain village around a shady square on the road up to the plateau.

**Krasi**
A village just off the road which claims to have the oldest plane tree in Europe, along with a 200-year-old Cretan house.

**Seli Ambelou Pass**
From here the windmills of the plateau can be seen in the pattern of the fertile plain below. One of the most spectacular views on the island.

**Tzermadion**
The biggest of the Lasithi villages, full of woven goods for sale and the access to the Trapeza Cave and the walk up to the Minoan site of *Karphi*.

**Psychro/Dikteian Cave**
The legendary birthplace of Zeus, a deep dark cave just above the village.

cave which is wrongly signposted. It lies 3km (2miles) inland above the village, not on the coast, and is reached on a dirt track. A small chapel stands near its entrance.

A torch is necessary to see anything in the cave. Minoan remains were discovered here but it is a place of pilgrimage today because of a revolt in 1823 against the Turks. Large numbers of Cretans sheltering in the cave were killed after being besieged here when guarantees of safe passage were not honoured.

From Milatos there is a quiet if winding drive through the mountains back towards Neapolis. Standing at the crossroads of several routes, **Neapolis** sees a lot of through traffic which occasionally stops at the roadside cafés around the central square. Here the visitor might try the local speciality, *Soumada* which is made from pressed almonds. Although it is a sizeable town with a population of 3,000, there is little to see other than a quiet park and a large, modern church which hosts a festival for the surrounding area on 15 August every year.

It does, however, have something of a history dating from Venetian times and was the seat of the Turkish governor of the province. Its most famous son was Petros Philargos who became Pope Alexander V in 1409 although he died in suspicious circumstances before he reached Rome.

The main new highway can be rejoined here or further excursions can be made inland. One of these is along the narrow road out of Neapolis towards Kastelli and Fourni; two quiet and pretty mountain villages. Off to the left is *Dreros* (*Driros*) 2km (1 mile) down a track, the site of an ancient Greek city state built around a market place. Also uncovered here was an early temple to Apollo and various significant inscriptions which gave important insights into the social and legislative structure of the society. As so often with these sites, much of it is overgrown and the casual visitor can gain very little impression of the place.

The road through Kastelli and Fourni offers an alternative route to Elounda and Spinalonga. When this road begins to descend, there are stunning views of the bay below and its distinctive topography, the sea being virtually enclosed by the larger island of Spinalonga.

**Elounda** is a growing resort, with all the facilities for the tourists who stay there, including a telephone office and English newspapers brought in every day. It remains very pretty around the harbour, which is still full of fishing boats. The views out to Spinalonga give it a very picturesque outlook and one of its proudest boasts is that it was the setting for the BBC TV series *Who Pays the Ferryman?*

*Inside the small chapel at Milatos*

*Old windmill towers at Elounda*

There is a road along a causeway to the large island and, on the right hand side as one goes away from Elounda, are the Venetian salt flats which are now only a stretch of muddy water. Crossing onto the Spinalonga Peninsula itself, one can follow the coast round to a small chapel, opposite which it may be possible to discern the remains of the sunken city of *Olous* which has not been excavated but is thought to date from the Classical Greek period.

The walk out along the causeway is an attractive one and it is possible to swim from here. The bridge crosses the channel which the French dug at the beginning of this century and converted the peninsula into an island.

**Spinalonga** proper is not this large island close to Elounda but ✳ the small island at the end of the bay. Boat trips are possible from most of the major resorts in the area. The Venetians built the fort in the sixteenth century, a military installation which was to thwart the Turks for many years after their capture of the mainland and was eventually ceded by a treaty. Until quite recently, the island was a leper colony (1903-1957); the last of its kind in Europe and clearly a place of much privation and cruelty. Houses and shops are still visible and some claim to have seen the occasional skull; it remains a very isolated, eerie place.

Elounda lacks any good beaches with the concrete stretch near the harbour not being a particularly attractive option and even the narrow strip of shingle along the causeway is not ideal. However, there are several reasonable beaches on the road heading north from Elounda, with the finest being at Plaka. The water is exceptionally clear and although the beach consists of large pebbles, this does not detract from the superb setting and the views out to Spinalonga Island. Plaka itself is a tiny village with a few tavernas and rooms to rent and is a very tranquil place to stay.

The road from Elounda to Ayios Nikolaos climbs into the cliffs above the sea, passing some hotels perched on the rocks but with no beaches accessible until the approaches to Ayios Nikolaos where development is intensive.

**Ayios Nikolaos** claims to be a sophisticated resort having grown up out of and retained the structure of a town which was an entity in itself before the tourists came, although a local population of 8,300 hardly gives it big-city status. Its setting is attractive, with impressive views out into the Gulf of Merabello and the mountains beyond. The worst of the strip development is stretched to either side of the town.

There is some evidence that the town was occupied by the Ancient Greeks, perhaps as the port for *Lato*, the Dorian city in the mountains. Information as to its role in the Roman and Byzantine period is scanty but the Venetians were definitely here, rebuilding the town and constructing a castle. The Turks also occupied it but this did not prevent the local population being active in supplying rebels in the numerous revolts against the Turkish occupation.

There are weekly ferries to Rhodes and Santorini and a bus station with frequent services to the other major towns on the island. The tourist office should have details of timetables and fares.

Traffic in the city is congested and the one way system is complicated. Finding places to park is also difficult; if all else fails, try in front of the sailing club at the far end of the harbour wall.

The town has all the usual tourist facilities and caters particularly for British tourists with the whole range of English newspapers prominent in all the kiosks. There are numerous souvenir shops containing local hand crafted items as well as the usual more downmarket mementoes. All of these tend to be more expensive than in other resorts.

Restaurants, cafés and discos are found around the harbour and the lake. They cater for British tastes in both the food and the entertainment they offer.

Accommodation for the independent traveller in Ayios Nikolaos is rare and there are few rooms to rent. It is very much a resort for those on package holidays and it is perhaps better to look for rooms in Elounda or nearby villages.

The harbour is the best place to start an exploration of the town with its various boats tied up at the quay and restaurants around it. Behind the harbour are streets leading inland with the usual range of souvenir shops.

A bridge leads over the channel cut to join the lake to the sea. Just opposite this bridge is the tourist information office which is well-organised and stages cultural events throughout the summer. Every 2 years, a big firework display is held as part of the celebrations for Naval Week which takes place in July.

Lake Voulismeni is the main feature of the town although it  doesn't really live up to the claims made for it. Locals claimed it was bottomless and it took an Englishman, Captain Spratt, to measure it at 64m (210ft) deep. The channel out to the sea is artificial and was dug in 1867 to clear the stagnant water which collected there. Claims that it is somehow volcanic and occasionally gives off fumes also seem without foundation; whether Artemis and Athena regularly bathed here is, of course, unverifiable. Nonetheless, the lakeside tavernas draw customers like a magnet, especially after dark.

It is possible to walk round most of the lake, passing some rather mangy caged birds on the way before climbing the steep cliff at one end from where there are good views of the lake.

A short distance inland from the lake, about 10 minutes walk uphill, is the Archaeological Museum. This consists of eight rooms  built around a courtyard in a modern building. There is an official guide on sale at the entrance and the finds are reasonably well-labelled. There is a rough chronological order, starting with Neolithic finds from caves and then moving on to the Minoan remains, including the Goddess of Mirtos libation vessel (a vase in the shape of a fat lady with an extremely long neck) and concluding with Graeco-Roman finds.

Room 1 contains Neolithic and Early Minoan finds from the cemetery at Ayia Photia near Sitia and potter's tools from the site at Mirtos on the south coast.

*Windsurfers at Plaka*

*The holiday resort of Ayios Nikolaos*

Room 2 displays the Goddess of Mirtos vessel, Minoan jewellery from Mohlos and tablets inscribed with Linear A script. There are also a large number of clay figurines which are typical finds from peak sanctuaries and were used as religious offerings.

Room 3 covers the Late Minoan period with pottery from the villa at Makriagalos and several finely decorated sarcophagi. The case in the centre of the room contains jewellery and ivory carvings.

Room 4 has less interesting finds from the period of the decline of the Minoan civilisation and are mainly artefacts from cemeteries. The most interesting exhibit is also the most macabre. The skeleton of a child is displayed exactly as it was found and can be examined in all its tragic detail.

Room 5 includes finds from the Classical period are exhibited in this gallery and include a large number of terracotta figurines from the sunken city of *Olous*.(Room 6 is the anteroom to room 5).

Room 7 displays finds from a Roman cemetery near Ayios Nikolaos and includes a skull which still has a gold wreath around it.

It is a reasonably interesting museum, bearing in mind the fact that all the best finds from the area have been put in Iraklion Museum.

There is no beach in Ayios Nikolaos unless the tiny patches of sand within the town count as such. There is a municipal beach near the bus station for which a small fee is charged. Almiros is a free beach about 2km (1mile) east of the town but all of these tend to get crowded and, if possible, it is better to go further afield or be satisfied with swimming from the rocks beyond the harbour.

In the hills behind Ayios Nikolaos there are three places worth a visit; the old church of Panayia Kera; the ancient site of *Lato* and the village of Kritsa. They are all on the road signposted Kritsa. About 1km ($^1/_2$ mile) before this village and about 8km (5miles) from Ayios Nikolaos, just off the road, is Panayia Kera. This is a church which dates from the thirteenth century and is famous for its frescoes of this period. The church is held to contain some of the finest examples of Byzantine art on the island.

It has three aisles, each with paintings from a different period and covering a different religious theme. The first aisle, as one enters, has some of the best-preserved paintings which are felt to show a tenderness and humanity lacking in some of the more stylised religious painting of the period. They tell the story of Anne, the Virgin's mother, her hopes for a child, the birth of Mary and her life leading up to the journey with Joseph to Bethlehem.

The central aisle contains the oldest paintings and these show a mixture of styles in their depiction of scenes from Christ's life. They include the Nativity; Herod's Massacre which shows a primitive style, and the Last Supper which is a more sophisticated painting.

The far aisle has pictures dealing with the Second Coming. It includes depictions of Paradise and hosts of angels along with various figures from the Old and New Testaments. Finally, there is a portrait of the founder of the church and his family which, although not very clear, is an interesting secular contrast to the religious paintings in the rest of the church.

The frescoes vary in quality but some are exceptionally well-preserved. As is the case with most of the old churches on the island, photography is not allowed inside the church. Postcards of the frescoes are available from the souvenir shop outside which also offers yoghurt with honey as refreshment.

Just as the one way system starts in Kritsa, there is a turning to the right which leads to the site of *Lato*, 3km (2miles) away on a reasonable dirt track from which there is a possible detour to the Kritsa Gorge.

On arrival at the site it is difficult to know which is the entrance; it is best to take the track which forks up to the right. Taking the lower path simply means scrambling up through the outer buildings of the town. However, this can be rewarding because the ruins become in-

# Places of Interest Beyond Malia

### Milatos
An old village 2km (1 mile) from the sea near a cave where numerous villagers were killed during a revolt against the Turks. Consequently, it is a place of pilgrimage today.

### Neapolis
A small town at the crossroads where most of the major roads in the area meet. It has a large church and a quiet park along with numerous roadside cafés.

### Elounda
One of the best resorts, built around a whitewashed fishing port in a spectacular setting looking out across to Spinalonga. A causeway leads out to the big island and the sunken city of *Olous* in an attractive walk.

### Ayios Nikolaos
The major resort in the region, it is lacking in beaches but does have a certain sophistication. At its centre is Lake Voulismeni around which are numerous cafés. Also of interest is the Archaeological Museum.

### Spinalonga
A small island with a Venetian fortress and a macabre recent history as a leper colony. Boat trips are possible from the resorts in the area.

### Plaka
A tiny village with a beautiful if stony beach, glorious water and views out to Spinalonga. An extremely tranquil place.

### Kritsa
A mountain village in an undeniably spectacular setting, it is now devoted to selling to the tourists and therefore has lost some of its attraction.

### Lato
The site of a Doric city with extensive remains of the town and the marketplace spreading all across the hillside. One of the more rewarding sites.

### Panayia Kera
One of the oldest churches on the island with well-preserved frescoes in each of its three aisles.

creasingly extensive and suddenly one arrives at the central market place and the site becomes recognisable as a town. The upper entrance leads straight into this central area.

Lato was a Doric city of some significance as can be seen by the extent of the city and the fortifications that were built around it. The centre of the town is at the top of the hill and offers good views down

*'Weaving hanging from every shop', Kritsa*

*The Byzantine church of Panayia Kera*

to Ayios Nikolaos. There are remains of workshops and houses and an impressive set of steps, perhaps some kind of theatral area. The variety and extent of the ruins make *Lato* one of the most rewarding sites on the island, though one of the least visited.

**Kritsa** is held to be the typical mountain village and, having featured in several major films, this seems to have gone to its head. Nowadays it is totally devoted to tourism, with expensive weaving hanging from every shop. It is best to park at the first car park on the way in to the village and walk because pandemonium then ensues in the narrow streets higher up and a car becomes a liability. Kritsa still has a certain interest but the village no longer represents the traditional way of life, for that the visitor simply needs to head into the mountains. The dirt tracks leading up into the mountains beyond Kritsa offer the possibility of interesting walks in isolated countryside.

# 3

# IRAKLION

Arriving in Iraklion (Herakleion) from the ferry terminal or the island's main airport, 4km ($2^1/_2$ miles) to the east, does not give the visitor the most agreeable first impression of the island. The city is undeniably dirty, noisy and overcrowded. Its modern concrete sprawl is partly the legacy of earthquake damage in 1926 and bombardment during The Battle of Crete in 1941. These allowed modern redevelopment to take place on a large and chaotic scale.

The city has a population of 102,000, making it the fifth largest city in Greece. Its rapid growth seems likely to continue, with figures showing Iraklion residents to have the highest per capita income in the whole of Greece. It thus proves a magnet for the poorer rural population.

There has been a settlement here since Neolithic times and the city probably served as a port for *Knossos* both in Minoan and Roman times, although few remains have been found within the city walls. In AD824 it was captured by the Saracens who renamed it *El Khandak* after the moat they dug around it. The modern street Khandakos follows the line of the medieval installation. During the Saracen occupation it became a well-known centre for piracy.

Numerous and bloody attempts were made by the Byzantine Empire to free the city but without success until AD961. The city was then regained by General Nikopharos Phokas. The whole island came under Byzantine control and remained so for over 200 years until Byzantium was threatened by Crusaders. The then ruler, Prince Boniface de Montferrat, more concerned about the fate of Constantinople, ceded the island to Venice for a thousand pieces of silver.

The Venetians took control of the whole island, despite much resistance and numerous revolts against their occupation. They made Iraklion their capital and named it *Candia*. This period marked a cultural revival on the island and the city became a centre for scholarly research. Painters flourished including Domenicos Theotokoupolis, whose icons can be seen in the church of Ayia Ekaterini, and El Greco who may have been born in Iraklion although Fodhele, a village to the east of the city, is firmly established on the tourist circuit for claiming that honour.

It is the Venetian legacy which most visibly dominates Iraklion, not only in the form of the huge city walls, which took over a century to complete, but also in the Loggia; a meeting place for nobles, the Arsenali dry docks and the Rocca al Mare fortress which guards the harbour.

Towards the middle of the seventeenth century, the Venetian Empire began to decline and in 1648 the forces of the Ottoman Empire began a siege of the city. It lasted 21 years, one of the longest in history and a testament to the strength of the Venetian defensive installations.

International help was sent in by sea because the city had gained a symbolic value, standing as the last outpost of Christendom under threat from the infidel. The French sent a force of 7,000 men but their leader, the Duke of Beaufort, was killed and the fleet limped home leaving the Venetians to continue to struggle alone. The final surrender took place in 1669 after 100,000 Turks and 30,000 Venetians had been killed.

The Turkish occupation was a source of even more resentment for the native Cretans than that of the Venetians, not least because of the forced conversion to Islam as illustrated by the number of mosques on the island. In Iraklion itself, the churches of Ayios Marcos and Ayios Titos were converted into mosques, only being rededicated at the beginning of this century.

Turkish rule continued uneasily and was opposed by a virtual guerilla war from 1820 onwards. Many of these revolts are commemorated in the street names of modern Iraklion, hence Odhos 1866 and Odhos 25 Avgostou.

From the union of Crete with Greece in 1913, Iraklion grew in size and importance and suffered heavily from the German bombardment in 1941; its port and airport making it a strategic objective for the invading forces.

After the war the city was extensively rebuilt and, in 1971, took over from Hania as the island's capital. The evidence of the oil storage tanks on the western approaches underlines the fact that Iraklion is the major port of entry to the island for both visitors and cargo. This has brought an obvious prosperity and increasing employment in new industry, the buildings for which are all too visible in the endless suburbs of the city.

While Iraklion may not be the most pleasant place to stay, it is worth a visit, not least to see the Archaeological Museum which houses all the important finds from the Minoan sites and helps considerably in any appreciation of these.

The visitor with a car might consider coming to the city on a Sunday. Although this has the disadvantage that many shops and some museums are closed (not the Archaeological Museum), the relative tranquillity of the weekend makes a visit much more pleasant with the considerable benefits both of less traffic and more available parking space.

There is a municipal car park in the moat just before one enters the city walls from the east or there maybe space in the Plateia Eleftherias, both conveniently close to the Archaeological Museum. Otherwise, parking is restricted to meters and it does seem that, unlike the rest of the island, parking rules are strictly enforced.

Iraklion offers the full range of accommodation possibilities although more effort may be required here in finding a room, especially at the cheaper end of the range than in other, more tourist based cities. It should be noted that staying in the centre of town is unlikely to offer peace and quiet.

Eating out here is reputedly expensive and the food mediocre but there are a large number of restaurants and cafés to choose from and it is possible to find a reasonable establishment. The best places to look are around the market off Odhos 1866, in the Plateia Eleftherias or Plateia Venizelou and along the harbour front.

In summer the city organises the Iraklion Summer Festival which offers a wide range of cultural events ranging from top international performers to displays of dancing by local schools. The programme has included performances by the Bolshoi Ballet, instrumental recitals, Greek plays and even recitals of the work of obscure Cretan Renaissance poets. There are also numerous exhibitions and impromptu puppet shows and other displays around the city.

Programmes should be available from the tourist office or the municipal offices and tickets can be purchased there or from special

*Street scene, Iraklion*

kiosks in Plateia Venizelou. Performances take place in open-air theatres, including the Koules, Venetian castle and other historic buildings of the city.

**Plateia Eleftherias** (Liberty Square) is where much of the traffic ✳ from the airport and the east of the island enters the city. It is a large, open square and its position high upon the defensive walls offers good views of the modern sprawl below. At its southern end, facing the public gardens, is a huge statue of Eleftherios Venizelos (1864-1936), the revered Cretan politician who was active in the Cretan Independence Movement and became Prime Minister of Greece. He is buried just outside Hania in a specially created memorial park. There are statues of Venizelos all over the island which are easily recognisable because of his striking resemblance to Lenin.

Opposite the statue are the **Public Gardens**, a peaceful place to escape the traffic which usually races round the square. In fact the square itself is, on closer inspection, quite green and pleasant, with trees and a bandstand at its centre.

The **Archaeological Museum** is the main attraction of this part of the city and lies at the northern end of the Plateia Eleftherias with its entrance on Xanthiou Dhidou opposite the tourist information office. The British Consulate is a short distance away on this road.

The museum is housed in a large and not particularly beautiful building dating from just before the war. The entrance fee is paid at a kiosk on entering the main gate and then you proceed into the building itself, passing the bookshop where detailed guides, postcards and other souvenirs can be bought.

The exhibits are displayed in twenty galleries on two floors and proceed in chronological order from Neolithic finds to Graeco-Roman to make a huge and undeniably impressive collection. It is an open question as to whether more might be gained from leaving the artefacts on the site where they were found. They might then be able to gain a context as well as add to the interest of these sites which can, in certain cases, seem denuded of all their treasures.

The labelling of exhibits is erratic and the cases may not always display what the official guide claims for them. A general outline of the contents of each gallery is given below along with the items of particular interest.

### Gallery 1

This covers the Neolithic period with examples of early stone art; various items of pottery with intricate designs of animals; several ivory figurines (case 13) and early jewellery. Most of the exhibits were found in tombs of the period or at *Knossos* underneath the Minoan palace.

### Gallery 2

This gallery contains finds from the Early Minoan Period (1900-

1700BC) including the earliest examples of Kamares style pottery with its distinctive red and white colouring. There are numerous clay figurines found in Peak sanctuaries (places of worship on mountain summits or in caves which revealed large numbers of offerings) and (case 25) the 'Town Mosaic' from *Knossos* which once served as a covering for a wooden box. This depicts several two- and three-storey houses and gives an extremely clear idea of what those at *Knossos* must have looked like.

### Gallery 3
Finds from *Phaestos* are exhibited here with more Kamares style pottery and (case 41) the famous *Phaestos* Disc, held to be the first example of printing with its impressed hieroglyphics on both sides. It has not been deciphered although theories abound as to its meaning, the most likely being that it is some kind of religious hymn.

### Gallery 4
This is one of the most interesting galleries in the museum, covering the period of the height of Minoan Civilisation (1700-1450BC). Many of the important finds from *Knossos* are displayed here including (case 51) the famous Bull's Head rhyton (a vessel for pouring libations). The right hand side is genuine but the left is restored. The ivory bull-leaper (case 56) illustrates an energetic Minoan sport. The figure looks incredibly agile with his limbs and muscles delicately depicted. The gaming board (case 57) found in 'The Corridor of the Draughtboard' presents evidence of less strenuous pursuits.

Other exhibits in this gallery include the royal mace (case 52) from Malia and the Snake Goddess figurines (case 50); female figures with snakes draped around them.

### Gallery 5
These finds date very much from the last days of Minoan power and the decline is apparent from the inferior quality of the art. The gallery contains mainly pottery with the Egyptian objects being of particular interest. These indicate that Egypt was a major trading partner for the Minoans. Also displayed here are examples of tablets bearing Linear A and Linear B script, some of which have been deciphered. The key to the script is preserved here; the tablets were some kind of register of the number of sheep, weapons etc in the palace.

## Gallery 6

This gallery contains artefacts from the cemeteries near *Knossos, Arhanes* and *Phaestos*. The most striking exhibit is perhaps the skeleton of a dismembered horse (case 75A) displayed as it was found, probably offered as a sacrifice to the dead. The number of weapons discovered in the tombs are seen as further evidence of the decline of the Minoans and the rise of the warlike Myceneans. The jewellery (case 87 and 88) is of gold and ivory and includes a famous gold seal ring from a royal tomb at *Knossos* which depicts in intricate detail a goddess and priestesses taking part in some religious rite in a field of lilies.

## Gallery 7

This seems to be the gallery where the labelling has gone most awry. It contains objects from the smaller villas and caves, as well as from the villa at *Ayia Triadha*. The Harvester's Vase (case 95) from the latter is decorated with a procession of men giving thanks for the harvest, the lower half of the vase is restored but the rest original. Another find from *Ayia Triadha* is the Chieftain's Cup (case 95) a vase on which is shown a prince listening to a report from an officer.

Also in the gallery are a large number of weapons and huge copper ingots each weighing 29.5kg (65lb) and thought to be units of exchange made from copper imported from Cyprus. The collection of jewellery includes the celebrated Two Bee Pendant (case 101) which was found near Malia.

On the wall are three huge double axes made of bronze found at *Nirou* just east of Iraklion. These double axes seem to have been an important symbol in Minoan religion and many have been found on sacred sites.

## Gallery 8

These are finds from the palace at *Zakros* in the far east of the island. The Rock Crystal rhyton (case 109) has been carefully reconstructed to show off the gold and ivory ring around the neck of the vase. There are several other rhytons including the fine Green Stone rhyton (case 111) along with various other vessels connected with religious rites.

## Gallery 9

Finds from the smaller sites in Eastern Crete from the period 1700-1450BC are displayed here. These are mainly pottery with a flask

*The Venetian Loggia, Iraklion*

from *Paleokastro* (case 120) displaying an octopus with a particularly endearing face. The other cases contain large numbers of clay figurines used as idols in worship.

## Gallery 10
This gallery covers the first Post Minoan period with the Mycenean influence visible in the much plainer style of the figurines.

## Gallery 11
A further decline in the standard of the artistry is visible here, along with the influence of a new style of pottery decoration which is called Geometric.

## Gallery 12
Here the evidence is of an eastern influence (hence the Orientalizing period) on the pottery and the jewellery. The latter shows some particularly intricate work (case 170) and was found in a tomb in the *Knossos* cemetery.

## Gallery 13

A distinct break in the collection is marked in this gallery and the display of sarcophagi provides a welcome contrast with the profusion of pottery which preceded it. The sarcophagi have two distinct forms; bathtub shapes, which were possibly used as such during the occupant's lifetime, and box shaped. They are uncomfortably small, due to the practice of burying people in a contracted, curled up position and are all decorated with various images of animals or in some cases of particular rituals.

Most guidebooks claim the wooden model of *Knossos* is displayed in this gallery but it has been moved upstairs where the next gallery is found.

## Galleries 14, 15 and 16

The whole of the upper floor is devoted to displaying the much restored frescoes from *Knossos*, *Ayia Triadha* and *Amnissos*. The subjects of the paintings are felt to give significant information about Minoan life. They consist mainly of naturalistic scenes of people and animals in everyday situations. Unlike representations of the other civilisations of this period, they do not depict military events and triumphs; this has led some to conclude that the Minoans were a peace-loving people.

To the left of the entrance of the gallery is the fresco from the Corridor of the Procession which depicts a group of young men advancing towards a goddess, with the figure known as the Cup Bearer being the most easily identifiable among them. Between the doors to the other galleries is the griffin fresco in distinctive red and white from the Throne Room at *Knossos*.

Beyond these are frescoes from the villa at *Ayia Triadha* and they include a naturalistic scene showing a cat about to pounce on some wild birds and a marine picture with dolphins and octopus.

On the opposite wall is the White Lilies and Red Irises fresco from *Amnissos*, the Bull Sports fresco from *Knossos*, the Partridge frieze, The Blue Ladies and, finally, the Prince with the Lilies fresco, all from *Knossos*.

In the middle of the gallery is the *Ayia Triadha* sarcophagus with its elaborate decorations on all four sides. The long sides depict funeral processions with offerings and sacrifices being made. The other two sides show chariots being pulled by griffins and horses.

At the far end of the gallery is a huge wooden model of the palace at *Knossos*, depicting how it was believed to be at the height of its influence. The size and extent of the palace are particularly clear and impressive from the model.

Gallery 15, to the left of the main gallery, contains smaller frescoes including the priestess dubbed by archaeologists *La Parisienne*, a detailed portrait of an individual woman. Gallery 16 contains the Blue Bird and Blue Monkey frescoes as well as the two interesting interpretations of the Saffron Gatherer; one as a boy, one as a monkey. This can only give ammunition to the sceptic who might wonder how accurate the reconstructions of these paintings are, given the limited original evidence available. In fact, all the frescoes were in very poor condition when discovered.

Many frescoes were revealed on the island of Santorini which showed direct Minoan influence and had been preserved by the volcanic ash. They are now in the Archaeological Museum in Athens.

## Galleries 17 and 18
These seem to have been closed for many years with various explanations given which range from staff shortages, lack of funds or restoration purposes. Gallery 17 contains the collection of a Doctor S. Yamalakis with artefacts from all periods. Gallery 18 contains exhibits from the Classical period.

## Gallery 19
Large works of art from the Classical period are displayed here along with examples of metalworking, the most impressive being the bronze shields.

## Gallery 20
The museum finishes with examples of Graeco-Roman sculpture, mainly statues without heads or feet.

The museum does have a café in the grounds and a number of benches in the garden where exhausted visitors can regain their energy before exploring the rest of the city.

From the Archaeological Museum there are numerous roads which head down into the heart of the city and the harbour. Alternatively, one can cross Plateia Eleftherias and continue west to the **Plateia** ✳ **Kornarou**, a quieter square with a Turkish fountain at its centre, housed in a fountain house which is now a café. Behind the Turkish fountain is a Venetian font known as the **Bembo Fountain** which is a curious mixture of Venetian and Roman styles dating from 1588. There is also a huge modern sculpture in the square called *Erotokritos and Aretousa*, inspired by the epic seventeenth-century poem *Erotokritos*, written by the Cretan Vincenzo Kornaros. Despite its obscure language, it was adopted by peasants who sing it out aloud. It is also often performed as part of the Iraklion Summer Festival.

**Odhos 1866**, named after the revolt against the Turks of that year, is the home of the street market and is one of the most atmospheric parts of the city. The stalls are spread along the street selling a whole range of provisions with the hubbub to match. In the alleys leading off on either side there are quieter cafés and tavernas.

At the end of this street is the central crossroads of Old Iraklion. The road bearing slightly to the right leads down to Venizelos Square, also accessible down **Daideilou** from Plateia Elftherias. The square is a focal point for tourists with its cafés grouped around the **Morosini Fountain** which was built in 1628 and named after the Venetian governor of the time. It is worth taking a closer look at this; the lions, which pre-date the structure by 100 years, are especially impressive.

Almost opposite the fountain is **Ayios Markos**, a Venetian church now looking rather squashed between the surrounding buildings. The church was first built in 1239 and was damaged several times by earthquakes and then rebuilt. Venetian governors who died on the island were buried here. It was converted to a mosque during the Turkish Occupation, when a minaret was added, and only reverted to Greek control in 1915 when the last Turks left the island. It was extensively restored in 1956 and now serves as a hall for concerts and exhibitions. Its opening hours depend on the functions going on that day. During the summer there are frequent exhibitions of paintings and sculpture.

Further down the road, on the left hand side, is a small park known as **El Greco Park** which has a statue of the painter at its centre. In summer, at the entrance to the park, there is a temporary post office and exchange service in its distinctive bright yellow portakabin. In Venetian times, the area around the park was the site of the noblemen's residences, including the Palazzo Ducale. However, nothing remains of these buildings.

The Venetian **Loggia** on the other side of the road has survived and is now restored and used for exhibitions. It was built in 1627 by

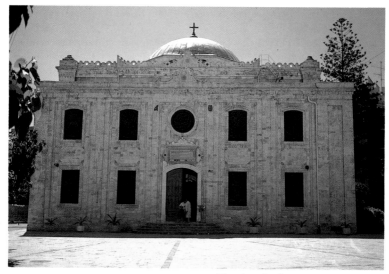

*The church of Ayios Titos, Iraklion*

Francesco Morosini. In Venetian times, it was a meeting place for the nobles of the city, while the Turks used it as a government building.

Just behind the Loggia is the **Dimarcheon**, the old Venetian armoury which is now used as the city hall. One one wall there are the remains of a Venetian fountain dating from 1602 which was placed here during the restoration of the building having being found in the foundations of the Loggia. Although much damaged, the figure of a woman, perhaps standing as the symbol for Crete, is still visible.

Slightly set back from the road in a quiet plaza is the church of **Ayios Titos**. The first church was built on this site in AD962 and was badly damaged several times during the Venetian occupation but was always rebuilt. On the arrival of the Turks it was converted into a mosque but was destroyed in the earthquake of 1856. It was rebuilt as a mosque and then reconverted into a church 50 years later, when the minaret was removed. Its most prized possession is a reliquary containing the skull of St Titus which was returned to the island from Venice in 1966. St Titus is particularly important on the island, especially in Iraklion where a procession is held every year on the

Saint's day. It is possible to visit the church but the usual dress rules apply ie: no shorts or bare shoulders.

The road **Odhos 25 Avgostou** is named after three martyrs killed by the Turks on 25 August 1898. On this road, which leads to the harbour, all the main travel agents and car hire firms can be found.

The inner harbour is full of yachts and small fishing boats and beyond, in the outer harbour, the bulk of the ferries which come back and forth from Athens daily are visible. A right turn at the end of Odhos 25 Avgostou leads down some steps to the Venetian **Arsenali**, the huge, vaulted dry docks, nowadays sandwiched between the modern blocks which characterise the city. The bus station for eastern destinations is a short walk along this road towards the ferry terminal.

The harbour wall stretches out to the Venetian fortress **Rocca Al Mare**, also known by its Turkish name of Koules, at the far end. This is open to the public despite the gates and the 'no entry' signs halfway along the wall.

The Arabs were the first to build a fort here in the ninth century which was followed by a Genoese construction in 1303 but this was destroyed in an earthquake. The fort seen today dates from 1523-1540, when the Venetians found themselves under increasing threat from the Turkish Empire and decided to improve the city's defences. Bearing in mind the length of the subsequent siege, it seems to have served its purpose well.

The fortress contains twenty-six rooms, some of them pitch black (the visitor is warned not to wander into these). However, the majority are light, vaulted chambers with the odd cannon carefully placed by the restorers. There is a steep, stony slope out to the battlements where plays are occasionally staged. Visitors can walk around the ramparts which provide magnificent views of the harbour and the Cape Tripiti to the west. The fort has been immaculately restored, perhaps leaving the construction a little too artificial for the tastes of some; whatever the arguments, it is well-worth visiting.

Turning back along the seafront away from the harbour, there are several restaurants and, opposite the Xenia Hotel, the **Historical and Ethnographical Museum**. This opened in 1953 and contains a miscellaneous collection which is not always well-labelled but covers the often neglected later periods of the island's history right up to the present day.

The basement contains fragments of Byzantine art and architecture; inscriptions from Turkish tombs and Venetian coats of arms. The ground floor has more Byzantine art with groups of icons and the representation of a chapel and its frescoes.

The first floor has memorabilia of the Cretan revolution and the Battle of Crete. One room represents the study of Nikos Kazantzakis and another deals with Manoli Tsouderos, the Cretan who was Prime Minister of Greece during the Battle of Crete.

The top floor contains the folklore collection, with examples of weaving, handicrafts and jewellery from the seventeenth to the nineteenth century. Such traditions continue today and handwoven items are often on sale to tourists in the mountain villages.

The remaining sites of interest, **Ayia Ekaterini Church** and **Ayios Minas Cathedral**, are in a small plaza, best reached by turning along Kolakerinous at the main crossroads (Nikopharos Fokos Square) and then turning left up any of the little alleys which lead off the main street.

The area is dominated by the huge Ayios Minas Cathedral, built in the nineteenth century and making up for what it lacks in beauty by its sheer size. It is one of the largest churches in Greece and can hold a congregation of 8,000. Just in front of the cathedral is a smaller church, this is the original Ayios Minas, a simple building which contains some eighteenth-century icons but which is usually locked.

On the other side of the square is Ayia Ekaterini Church which houses a museum of religious art, mainly a collection of icons. The icon painters flourished during the Venetian period forming a distinctive school the focus of which is Mihailis Damaskinos, a probable contemporary of El Greco although with a very different style. There are six icons by Damaskinos in the collection which were originally kept at the Vrondisi Monastery south of Iraklion. The church itself was built in 1555 but has later additions to it, most noticeably the elegant seventeenth-century doorway. It served as an important school for painting and theological study during the Venetian period.

The **City Walls** dominate Iraklion and it is possible to walk the 4km ($2^1/_2$ miles) of their perimeter although this is not always easy and can involve a certain amount of scrambling about on rough ground. The road also follows the inside of the walls and this can be an interesting drive if there is not too much traffic; stops can be made to look at the old gates.

Construction of the walls by the Venetians began in 1462 and was

*The Venetian Arsenali*

supervised by the military engineer, Sammichele. Although there were earlier Byzantine walls, the growth of the city rendered these inadequate. The new walls took over a century to build and they are extremely thick in places but obviously proved their worth during the Turkish siege. They are very well-preserved, as are two of the original gates. To the west is the Hania Gate, built in 1570, which still has elaborate carvings as does the Kainouria Gate at the end of Odhos Evans.

There are seven bastions along the walls; the Martinegro Bastion is the southernmost and overlooks the football ground. This is the site of the **Grave of Nikos Kazantzakis** (1883-1957) and bears the inscription in Greek, 'I hope for nothing. I fear nothing. I am free.' He could not be buried in a church cemetery because of his unorthodox religious views. The controversy still rumbles over these with the film adaptation of *The Last Temptation of Christ* which has taken over from *Zorba the Greek* as his best-known work.

Real Kazantzakis fans will want to visit Kazantzakis Street, where he was born. It is a street full of old houses with typical Turkish balconies. It is ironic that the site of his house is now a modern block

*The harbour and fortress, Iraklion*

of flats while less illustrious houses remain.

Just outside the city walls, below the bastion, is a small zoo. This only has a few animals but provides the visitor with the unusual opportunity of seeing the rare kri-kri wild goat.

## Beaches

The most accessible beaches are those beyond the airport to the east of the city along the old Ayios Nikolaos road. Although they are not unpleasant, their proximity to the airport can make for noisy sunbathing. However, those easily bored with the beach might find plane spotting an interesting diversion.

Nea Alikarnassos has a municipal beach, so there is a charge to use it. It is no better than the free beaches further along the coast but it does have showers.

*Amnissos* is perhaps a better choice, it has a reasonably long beach and a few tavernas. It is also a well-known Minoan site as a port of *Knossos* mentioned by Homer in the *Odyssey*. A two-storey villa was also uncovered here which contained several frescoes now on display in Iraklion Museum. The site is fenced off and little can be seen by the public.

A short distance further along the road is Tombrouk Beach, a sandy stretch with a few tavernas on the road behind. The road continues very close to the coast and the shore is easily accessible in most parts to unnamed beaches. (For further information on this coastline see the Iraklion to Ayios Nikolaos chapter.)

The beaches west of the city are more difficult to reach, partly because of the large hotels which block access to the sea. Amoudhara Beach is the best-defined public stretch of sand but even this is difficult to get to. Further problems are caused by the increasing spread of industry out to these suburbs which does nothing to enhance the view.

## Excursion from Iraklion to the Island of Santorini (Thera)

There are scheduled services to the island from Iraklion but boats also go from other north coast ports as part of day trips organised by travel agencies. The boat journey takes about 5 hours.

**Santorini** is 100km (60 miles) north of Crete and many recent archaeological finds have shown strong links between the people who lived here and the Minoans. There is a theory that a huge

# Places of Interest in Iraklion

**Plateia Eleftherias**
A busy square on the city walls containing the public gardens and the Archaeological Museum.

**Archaeological Museum**
A huge museum with all the significant finds from sites on the island, including frescoes from *Knossos*, vases and jewellery.

**Plateia Kornarou**
A pleasant square with Turkish and Venetian fountains.

**Odhos 1866**
The street market of Iraklion, selling food, leather and other provisions.

**Plateia Venizelou**
A pleasant square with cafés grouped around the Morosini Fountain.

**Ayios Markos**
A restored Venetian church now used as a concert and exhibition hall.

**Loggia**
The old Venetian meeting place for nobles, now elegantly restored.

**Kazantzakis' Grave**
Tomb of the controversial author of *Zorba the Greek* and *The Last Temptation of Christ*, much honoured by his native land.

**Ayios Titos**
An impressive church with a long and chequered history, now contains the skull of St Titus.

**Arsenali**
The huge arches of the Venetian dry docks, looking out over the harbour.

**Fortress (Rocca al Mare)**
The Venetian defence against invasion from the sea, now much restored and open to the public offering good views of the harbour.

**Historical and Ethnographical Museum**
Houses a miscellaneous collection covering the Byzantine, Venetian and Turkish period of the city as well as photographs of the Battle of Crete.

**Ayia Ekaterini**
A small, old church with a collection of icons and religious art.

**Ayios Minas**
The huge cathedral, the seat of the Bishop of Crete, built in the nineteenth century with the original Ayios Minas Church in the square below.

**City Walls**
A 4km ($2^{1}/_{2}$ mile) perimeter wall around the city, still a major landmark.

Iraklion harbour

volcanic explosion on the island may have been the reason for the great catastrophe which destroyed the Minoan civilisation in 1450BC. It has been calculated that any such eruption would have been many times stronger than that of Krakatoa and the subsequent tidal wave could easily have engulfed Crete.

Excavations on the island revealed buildings of up to three storeys and numerous frescoes which had been very well-preserved by the volcanic ash. In fact, a whole town was revealed at Akrotiri, prompting comparisons with Pompeii. Buses run a regular service from Thira to the site. There are also Roman remains in Thira itself.

It is not just the archaeology which brings visitors here but the volcano. The old crater now forms the harbour and volcanic fumes can be seen coming from the two islets in the bay. There are also organised trips to visit hot springs. The black sand and volcanic rock in the fields give the whole island a very distinctive and impressive landscape.

The main town of **Thira**, where most visitors will arrive, is high up on the cliff above the harbour and reaching it involves a steep climb or engaging the services of a donkey. It is clearly one of the most picturesque places in the Mediterranean, with its whitewashed houses in such a spectacular setting. This situation is now extensively exploited by and for tourists. In summer the large number of visitors on day trips can mean that the place is rather crowded.

# 4

# *SOUTH OF IRAKLION*

In archaeological terms, the region south of Iraklion is the richest on the island, containing the two most important Minoan palaces at *Knossos* and *Phaestos*, a Roman town at *Gortyn* and numerous minor sites. In the south, the flat, fertile Messara Plain allows easy access to certain parts of the coast, access denied by the mountains in other regions.

The area does not offer the most spectacular views on the island, not having a high mountain range, but it is precisely these gentler contours that have fostered such extensive population development throughout history and given the region such a crucial role in the island's past.

## *Knossos*

*Knossos* is, of course, the most visited historical site on the island both by those who have a keen interest in archaeology and those who deem the visit more of a cultural duty. It is likely that the former will be distressed by the controversial reconstruction of the palace which took place during the early excavation, while the latter may be somewhat comforted by it. John Pendlebury, the British archaeologist who worked on the site, claimed in one of his works, 'without the reconstruction the palace would be a meaningless heap of ruins.' However, others disagree and argue that the reconstruction is simply the addition of artificial ruins to the real ones. Like so much else relating to *Knossos*, the argument continues among experts and laymen alike.

To reach the site from the centre of Iraklion, visitors should head north of Plateia Eleftherias and turn left at the roundabout to pass alongside the Public Gardens and out of the city walls. Eventually, this road will join that leading to *Knossos*. Within Iraklion itself the site is poorly signposted but once you are on the right road, the palace is reached rapidly, being only 5km (3miles) from the city centre. The site is marked by a collection of buildings that have grown up to serve the numerous visitors. Unfortunately, the food here is poor and expensive and the goods on sale in the souvenir shops fail to emulate the artistic endeavour of their ancestors . There is one set of rooms to rent, up the hill, but the whole development is deserted once the palace has closed.

The actual site is on the other side of the road with a car park in front of it. It is open from 8am to 7pm and is obviously quieter early and late when the coach parties can be avoided. As well as organised trips, there are frequent scheduled buses from Iraklion which stop outside the site.

*Knossos* is clearly the key to Minoan civilisation both now and in the period when it was at the height of its power. It plays a central role in many of the Greek myths. The most famous of these include that of Theseus and the Minotaur and Dedalus and Icarus. Dedalus was Minos' chief engineer and his ill-fated flight was prompted by Minos' displeasure over the incident with Theseus. Theseus, the Athenian King's son, was to be one of the annual intake of sacrifices to Minos. Guided by the thread supplied by Ariadne (Minos' daughter) he found his way through Dedalus' maze, killed the Minotaur and ran off with Ariadne, only to abandon her later.

There are also references to the palace in Homer's *Odyssey* which further underline the city's importance. However, this has also raised controversy over the dating of the settlement as Homer was writing several centuries after the Minoan period. The chronology of the palace is still dogged by heated archaeological debate and one view even claims that the major civilisation at *Knossos* was not that of the Minoans but was of a much later period and the work of the Myceneans from mainland Greece.

Most archaeologists do, however, accept that it was the Minoans who were the force behind *Knossos*. The term Minoan is one invented by archaeologists to classify this particular period and does not signify a particular race of people. It does seem likely that there was a man behind the Minos myth; a powerful king who had his power base at *Knossos* and from here dominated the whole Aegean. This power was clearly not military alone. The evidence of the frescoes and the artistry of the pottery shows a high degree of cultural sophistication which was disseminated throughout the region.

There is further controversy over the question as to whether Minos was a ruthless tyrant or a more progressive, benevolent ruler. The evidence is inconclusive but it is clear that the people who lived at *Knossos* enjoyed a prosperity far removed from the primitive neolithic hunter gatherers who preceded them. Their occupation of such vulnerable coastal sites suggests that either they dominated the region to such an extent that they had no enemies to fear, or that they were a peace-loving people.

What the visitor sees is essentially the palace and the central residences of the courtiers. However, the site is much more extensive than this, both in the area it covers; once having supported a population of 80,000 in an area of 22,000m² (26,000yd²) and in the period of time in which it was inhabited.

Neolithic remains have been found below the central court of the palace. The fact that every period of settlement is built on top of that which preceded it was a fundamental problem for the early excavation. The site is extremely deep and at one point the mining expertise of two of the excavators became crucially important. The reconstruction of the palace was undertaken partly for this reason, each layer that was uncovered had to be shored up in order to allow further excavation below. Today the visitor has the same problem as the archaeologist in trying to gain a picture of how the palace looked at each stage of its settlement.

The Bronze Age marked the real growth of the Minoan civilisation, with the first palaces being built around 1900BC. These were then destroyed by earthquakes some 200 years later and rebuilt in 1700BC to be known as the New Palaces. A final catastrophe, the nature of which has not been established, occurred in 1450BC and the Minoan civilisation began to wane, although there is evidence that *Knossos* was reoccupied after this destruction. These new occupants were probably Mycenean invaders, described as squatters by Arthur Evans, rather than the remaining Minoans who retreated into mountain settlements.

Excavations started at the beginning of this century although the site was identified earlier in 1837 by Robert Pashley, the English explorer. It was not until Schliemann's excavations of Troy that interest was renewed in *Knossos* and, even then, various political

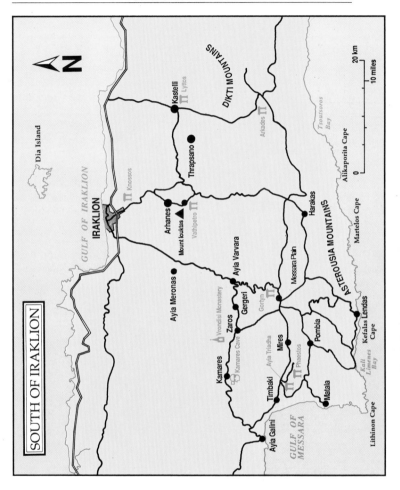

problems with the Turks prevented work starting. Then the dynamic force of the Englishman Arthur Evans (1851-1941) arrived on the scene. He bought the site and financed a whole team of excavators to work there which meant that, until the war, the site was very much a British preserve.

Evans had a very strong, somewhat eccentric personality, best detailed in Dilys Powell's book *The Villa Ariadne*; the villa was the house Evans built and the headquarters of the excavations. He had very distinct ideas about the site and the nature of the Minoan civilisation he uncovered. His reconstructions and theories have been bitterly attacked by other archaeologists. Clearly, his obsession with the place and his very personal theories, combined with a rather autocratic style, upset many scholars and, at times, the Greek authorities. Nonetheless, it is his statue that marks the entrance to the palace and it was his persistence and finance that allowed the site to be fully developed and reveal the previously unknown Minoan civilisation.

The palace is confusing because of its multitude of layers and the lack of official signs or labels of its different parts. It is possible to employ a guide and go round in a group but the guides vary both in the extent of their knowledge and their command of English and it is very much a matter of personal preference whether their services are used.

The independent visitor may find it better not to try and follow a prescribed route but simply to wander around the various buildings and pick up the points of interest in this way. No route will be offered here but rather an account of the main structures which are visible.

At the entrance to the palace is a bookshop where official guides are on sale which obviously contain more detailed information than can be given here. They are reasonably reliable and written by reputable Greek archaeologists although their detailed commentaries can lead to confusion and complication.

The visitor enters through the **West Court** which was the original ceremonial entrance and served as some kind of meeting place or perhaps the market. The first objects the visitor will notice are three circular storage pits common in all the Minoan palaces, perhaps used as grain silos or, at certain times, as rubbish tips.

It is here, in the court, that the bust of Evans is placed, recognition which he particulalrly appreciated. Despite his brushes with Greek authority, he is also remembered by having a street named after him in Iraklion, Odhos Evans.

The visitor should try to locate and enter through the **Corridor of the Procession**. This is a raised walkway where the procession fresco was found, part of which is copied and reproduced a little further into the palace. Also visible are the huge horns of consecration which have obviously been much reconstructed. These representations of the bull's horns were apparently common in the palaces, the bull being a sacred animal for the Minoans.

As with all the Minoan palaces, it is the Central Court which dominates and all construction is around this; hence the four wings, north, south, east and west. This is the easiest place for visitors to get their bearings. It is a paved area 50m by 25m (164ft by 82ft) and was probably the site of religious ceremonies or even the sport of bull leaping which was depicted on so many of the artefacts found here.

The myth of the labyrinth in which the Minotaur was kept is central to the palace of *Knossos* but nothing has been uncovered of such a maze. Some theories claim that it was the palace itself that was the labyrinth and the bulls were chased through it to the Central Court. Other theories focus on the etymology of the word. *Labrys* means double axe in Greek and the symbol of the double axe has been found inscribed all over the palace, suggesting a religious significance which may somehow tie up with the Minotaur myth.

The Upper Floor on the west side of the court is reconstructed and was called the Piano Nobile by Evans. It is thought that this could even have been the fifth floor of the original palace. Up here is a tricolumnar shrine, some reconstructed frescoes including the Ladies in Blue and the Blue Monkey. Also visible are the **West Magazines**; the huge lines of storage space for the giant pithoi jars, these 18 storerooms could contain about 400 jars. The majority of these are thought to have contained oil which fuelled the flames of the fire which accompanied the final destruction of the palace. In several rooms, the blackened stone testifies to the ferocity of this fire.

Descending from here on the left of the Central Court is the **Throne Room**. This is now closed off but still contains the gypsum throne as it was found, along with the imposing red and white frescoes of the griffon, and an intricately patterned floor. These are visible by peering over the barrier from the anteroom where there is a wooden replica of the throne.

The **East Wing** contains some of the most interesting rooms in the palace which are best reached down the **Grand Staircase**. This is now covered with an ugly modern roof but is still an imposing structure which was clearly specially designed to allow the light from the stairwell to illuminate the rooms below. The Minoan pillars were made of wood and those seen today are reconstructions. The staircase leads to the **Kings Hall**, also known as the Hall of the Double Axes because of the symbols found scratched onto the wall. Half of

*Large storage jars in the ruins at* Knossos

the room is fenced off but even in its original use it was meant as a multipurpose chamber, sections of which could be closed off to alter its size. There is another replica wooden throne here.

Following the corridors, the visitor reaches the **Queens Hall** which is somewhat smaller and contains a copy of the Dolphin fresco. Of particular interest is the **Queen's Bathroom**, complete with clay bath and the Queen's Toilet. This has various drainage pipes visible which allowed for running water and flushing toilets in the palace, feats which modern Greek plumbing sometimes seems to find hard to emulate.

There is a whole Upper Floor on top of these Royal apartments which to a large extent mirrors the rooms below and includes another bathroom and one of several Lustral Basins found around the palace. A Lustral Basin is a kind of bath but archaeologists feel they occupy too public a position to have been used for this purpose and therefore are assumed to have been places for ritual anointing in religious ceremonies. Workshops were also found in this eastern section, along with a room Evans called the schoolroom because of the way the benches were arranged within it, although this too was

*Fresco at* Knossos

probably a workshop.

The north section of the palace contains the **Corridor of The Draughtboard** where the games board was found. This leads out to the **North Gate** and the carefully reconstructed and much photographed Leaping Bull fresco with the distinctive red pillars around it.

Other parts of the palace worth looking for are the **South House**, sited as the name suggests and presumably the house of a top-ranking official and, at the opposite end of the site, the **Theatral Area**. This is a paved court from where the **Royal Road**, a paved pathway, leads away from the palace to the town of *Knossos*. It is thought this path was lined with houses and led to the Little Palace, a smaller version of *Knossos*. This, along with the various other smaller buildings in the vicinity, such as the Caravanserai and the Temple Tomb, are not open to the public.

Beyond *Knossos* the road leads up into the mountains where there are several villages of interest. Only a few minutes drive from *Knossos*, there is an aqueduct which was built by the Egyptians in their very brief period of influence here in the early part of the last century.

The road then reaches **Arhanes**, a town of some size, although surprisingly lacking in shops and other such facilities as are most of the mountain villages in the region. They are seemingly served by travelling salesmen who tour the region in vans fitted with loudspeakers announcing their presence from great distances. The town also has a one-way traffic system which can be very confusing.

Evans not only excavated *Knossos*, he also found Minoan remains here in Arhanes. There are three sites in and around the town, none of which are officially open but visitors can peer through the fences. The first is *Phourni*, a Minoan cemetery where jewellery and other offerings were found in the tombs. The second consists of the remains of a town over which the modern Arhanes was built. Most significant of all is the religious site of *Anemospilia* which is 3km (2miles) away in a westerly direction.

This latter site was only discovered in the last 10 years. It is important because the shrine seems to have been destroyed by an earthquake midway through a ceremony in which a human sacrifice was taking place. This jolted the view that many had previously held of the Minoans as highly civilised, advanced people. Although animal sacrifices had frequently been found, few had wanted to believe that they did the same to humans.

The theory is that the rite was one last attempt to avert an impending catastrophe and a young man was sacrificed on the altar. The intricately inscribed knife was found near his body and some of his blood had been drained off. However, soon after the victim's death, the catastrophe came anyway, in the form of an earthquake. This killed the priest who had just carried out the ceremony and his skeleton was found across the room. Although controversial at the time, examination by anthropologists, pathologists and the archaeologist mean the view that it was a human sacrifice is no longer in doubt.

There are a few churches of interest in the area including one in the town's central square. The best frescoes are found in the church of Ayios Mikhail Archangelos at **Asomatos** which is 3km (2 miles) on a dirt track from Arhanes. The frescoes date from the early fourteenth century but finding the key for this building can be a problem; someone at the café in Arhanes may be able to help.

From Arhanes, a road heads into the mountains before petering out into a dirt track which passes the tiny church of Ayia Ani. This is a scene typical of the island; a new chapel in an isolated position, probably only used once a year on the relevant Saint's day.

Just beyond here is a track up to the summit of Mount Iouktas (Yiouchtas) which overlooks the region at a height of 811m (2,660ft). Near the summit is a large Minoan peak sanctuary which even had a Minoan road leading up to it. The site is now fenced off. At the summit itself is another little chapel, this one dedicated to Aphendis Christos and an annual pilgrimage to the church takes place on 6 August. However, the most frequent story told about this mountain is that it is the burial place of Zeus and the shape of the mountain is supposed to resemble the profile of a man. All this is undermined by the fact that Zeus was supposed to be immortal.

The lower track curves round away from the mountain to **Vathipetro** which is periodically signposted and the drive, though rough, isn't too bad. The site is just off the road, about 100m (330ft) away. A Minoan villa is located here which is open to the public although some of the rooms may be locked.

Various shrines and storerooms were found on the site, with the latter being of most interest. Many original tools and farming implements were found in place here. These included sixteen giant pithoi storage jars and a well-preserved wine press which indicates that the mechanics of grape pressing used today were the same 3,000 years ago. It is these tools that are visible if the rooms are unlocked; otherwise the visitor will have to peer through the windows or simply enjoy the view.

It is possible to complete a circuit by following the track round to Houdetsi where it rejoins a tarmac road and passes through several quiet mountain villages. Following the signs from Peza in the hills north of here takes you to the village of **Mirtia** (sometimes known by its old name of Varvari). It is distinguished by the huge and multilingual signs advertising the Nikos Kazantzakis Museum. These demonstrate the way to the village very effectively but, at the final, crucial turning, they disappear. If the visitor has to drive round the village, it is not time wasted because it is an extremely pretty place with a profusion of flowers in every garden and on every balcony, even at the height of the dry summer.

The museum offers a detailed account of Kazantzakis' life, including his various periods abroad, with a large number of documents relating to his book *Zorba the Greek*. It is clear he was controversial in his own time and controversy haunts him beyond the grave with the recent film adaptation of *The Last Temptation of Christ*. Kazantzakis' grave is on the city walls in Iraklion.

Another interesting place in this region is reached by heading east and then turning off the main road to the Angarathos Monastery which was built by the Venetians in the sixteenth century. It became known as a major scholarly institution and training ground for leading churchmen. When the Turks invaded, its numerous valuable treasures and icons were taken to the island of Kythera. The current church dates from the nineteenth century but several of the older buildings survive and can be seen from the courtyard. These can be identified by their sixteenth-century inscriptions.

**Voni**, on the opposite side of the valley, is known for its shrine to Ayia Marina; 1km ($^1/_2$ mile) beyond the village. This consists of a large modern church with the shrine and icons in a small chapel below. There is a residential courtyard here because the place is known for its miracle cures. Those suffering from a range of different maladies come and stay in the rooms here in the hope of recovery.

**Thrapsano** is the next village along the road and is a centre for the production of ceramics. The workshops are on the approaches to the village, with their distinctive big red pots and urns displayed outside. There is very little to see or stop for in the village itself.

There are a few other very small villages in the region like Evangelisomo (Evangelismos) and Sklaverokhori which are famous for their churches and early frescoes.

The road then reaches **Kastelli**, 8km (5miles) from Thrapsano; something of a contrast to what has gone before. It has a bank, post office and some clothes shops with highly fashionable attire displayed, as well as a couple of supermarkets and cafés. It once had a Venetian castle, which accounts for its name, but nothing of this remains.

From Kastelli there is a reasonable if narrow road down to the north coast which passes the little village of Pigi; *pigi* means spring in Greek and the place was known in Graeco-Roman times for its curative waters. There is also a tenth-century Byzantine church in an attractive setting. It is constructed in distinctive brown stone with early frescoes inside. However, these are not particularly well-preserved.

The north coast area is described in the Iraklion to Ayios Nikolaos chapter.

A rough track leads from Kastelli to Xidas and from here to the ancient site of *Lyttos* which was a powerful and belligerent city state in Classical times. It flourished under the Romans after putting up strong resistance to their occupation. However, there is little left of the city today and the excursion is only made worthwhile by the views it offers down to the coast.

Heading south of Kastelli, there are few places of particular interest although it is a pleasant drive through the hills. **Arkalohori** is the biggest town in the region but even here there is little for the tourist to see, as it is a centre for local farmers and caters purely for their needs.

However, it does have something of a history, being mentioned in a Venetian census of 1583. Its church dates from that period and nearby is a cave where votive offerings and bronze axes were found. Some make yet another claim that it is the birthplace of Zeus but it is not established on the tourist circuit as such. *Arkades*, a site to the south-east, was an important city state where a few late tombs have been found but it was destroyed by the Romans and, as with so many of the sites, little of the city remains.

Eventually, any of the roads heading south will reach the more major east-west route which is not quite finished. There is a section between Demati and Kato Kastelliana which is unpaved but this is a passable if a very slow drive.

The coast is accessible in very few places from this road. The only feasible option is to head down to Tsoutsouras and even this is difficult, the dirt track being very rough and long.

Heading west on the road, one passes through Pirgos and then onto the **Messara Plain**, the largest fertile area on the island. It is 30km (18$^1$/$_2$ miles) in length and 5km (3 miles) wide and in ancient times was a wheat growing area but now supports a wide range of crops. The region has always been prosperous and encouraged settlement, with the result that substantial archaeological finds have been made here.

To reach the plain, most visitors will probably not come from the east but rather come across the island directly from Iraklion, a trip which should take less than 1 hour, being only around 60km (37miles) on a reasonable road.

The road which leaves the suburbs of Iraklion and is signposted to *Phaestos* is not one of the most interesting or attractive drives on the island but is a rapid journey. A more rewarding route is to take the minor road up to Voutes, Ayia Meronas (Aghios Miron) and Prinias, before rejoining the main road at Ayia Varvara.

The minor road passes through a number of pretty mountain villages including **Ayia Meronas** which is on the ancient site of *Ravkos*. It has a an underground chapel built in the grotto of the third-century St Meronas who was a bishop of the island. He was known for his ability to work miracles. The most famous of these was when he killed a dragon by throwing a stone at it, this caused an avalanche which crushed the beast. Apparently, there is still a huge rock near the village which is meant to roar when there is going to be a hard winter; giving rise to the local saying 'the dragon is coming'. The modern church is built on top of the cave and is visible from the road.

A short distance away, just outside Prinias, are some manmade caves cut out of the rock and a number of tombs were found nearby, containing both Minoan and much later Roman graves. The village is close to the site of the Classical city state of *Rhizenia* (*Risinia*) and two Greek temples have been found here, along with friezes depicting various animals and goddesses. These are now in Iraklion Museum. The site is fenced and not easy to find and it is perhaps best to ask in the village for directions to the path.

**Ayia Varvara** stands at the crossroads of this area and sees a large amount of traffic. Because of this, it is dusty and has little to recommend it, although it is a good place to pick up supplies of fruit. Its claim to fame is the small chapel perched on a rock which is said to be the *Omphalos*, or belly button, of Crete.

From Ayia Varvara there is another detour further west into the mountains. This route arrives, after a pleasant if winding drive, at **Gergeri** which has a memorial to twenty-five partisans who were killed during the war. Zaros is the next village and is split in two parts; Ano Zaros and Kato Zaros.

A few kilometres beyond Zaros and 1km ($^1/_2$ mile) off the main road is the Moni Vrondisi, high up on the hillside with good views down to the coast, even if it is somewhat windswept. Outside is a fifteenth-century fountain built by the Venetians. Inside the church (a monk will unlock the door) there are some early frescoes which are seen as particularly fine examples of their type. The monastery used to house an extensive collection of icons by Damaskinos, a sixteenth-century Cretan icon-painter who moved to Venice. These icons are now in The Ayia Ekaterini Museum in Iraklion.

At the village of Vorizia there is a track to the abandoned Valsamonero Monastery. The church should be open from 8am to 1pm but it might be wise to check at the warden's house which is at the start of the track. The monastery is 2.5km ($1^1/_2$ miles) away. All that remains of the monastery is the church of Ayios Phanourios which has an unusual combination of Venetian and Byzantine styles. It has three aisles; the northern one is felt to be the original four-teenth-century construction while the other two were added later. They contain fifteenth-century frescoes depicting, among others, the Virgin, St John and Christ.

**Kamares**, 3.5km (2miles) further along the tarmac road from Vorizia is an undistinguished village but the starting point for a climb into the hills to see the Kamares Cave. This is a difficult walk which will take at least 4 hours and, although marked, the route is not easy to find. The cave contained the distinctive Kamares pottery with its reddy brown markings and was another early religious sanctuary. Other walks in the hills are possible from here, including climbing Mount Ida — the highest mountain in Crete, at 2,456m (8,056ft).

From Kamares the road turns down to the coast and the holiday resort of Ayia Galini. Otherwise, return to Ayia Varvara and follow the road down to Ayia Deka.

**Ayia Deka** (Aghii Deka) is named after ten martyrs who were

*Ayios Titos church*, Gortyn

*The Roman theatre at* Gortyn

*An intricately-carved
statue at* Gortyn,
*now protected from
the elements*

beheaded by the Romans in the third century for refusing to worship Roman Gods. Their tombs can be found in the small modern chapel on a track west of the village.

It is not, however, Ayia Deka which most visitors come to see but the Roman site of *Gortyn* (*Gortys*). This is just west of the village and is easily visible from the road. There is a car park in front of it.

π   *Gortyn*, recognised principally for its Roman remains, was in fact an important Classical city known for its wars with *Knossos* and even before that as the mythical site where Zeus brought Europa. *Gortyn* took the side of the invading Romans in 67BC and was rewarded by being made the island's capital during this period. It was visited by Hannibal on his way to Africa.

Later it became an important Christian centre and the church of Ayios Titos which dominates the site is one of the earliest on the island. St Titus was sent here as a bishop by St Paul who seemed to think that the Cretans were in severe need of his help to redeem their supposedly flawed characters. Titus spread the word but was then martyred and his bones are now in Ayios Titus Church in Iraklion, having been returned to the island by the Venetians in 1966. Gortyn was then destroyed in AD824 by the Saracen invaders.

The site covers a much wider area than that which is fenced off for visitors. It spreads to the other side of the road and the hill above and these unmarked sites repay further investigation.

Within the main site is a small museum with about a dozen statues. The main items of interest are, however, at the other side of the entrance kiosk. The church of Ayios Titos probably dates from the seventh century and has three aisles with one side now open to the elements. In one of the aisles there is still a shrine decorated by locals with candles and other offerings to Ayios Titos. However, the others seem to be distinguished only by being inhabited by large numbers of birds.

In front of the church is the Roman Forum area from where the path leads to the Odeum. This is easily recognisable as a theatre, with its tiers of precariously shored up seats overlooking a flat stage area. Behind the theatre is the most significant find from the site. It is enclosed in a covered building and is therefore only visible by peering in from the side. Inside are the stone tablets which constitute the *Gortyn* law code. The first fragment of the code was found by a visiting French scholar in 1857, in the mill stream above the site. It was deciphered and found to relate to the adoption of children.

Further fragments were then discovered by chance when the mill stream was drained, revealing twelve inscribed tablets in all.

On deciphering the Doric Greek, which reads from right to left on one line, then left to right on the subsequent line, the whole foundation of a legal system was uncovered. This gave great insights into the social system of the time, revealing some quite progressive ideas including the statement, 'If a husband and wife should be divorced she is to have her own property which she came with to her husband,' provided the divorce was not her fault. Other topics dealt with at some length were the details of property and inheritance rights as well as the fines for rape or adultery, all of which mean that the find is one of the most significant and revealing made on the island.

Above the site, after a 10 minute climb, are the remains of the acropolis, with a mixture of Minoan, Greek and Roman remains. The most rewarding area, however, is across the main road where there are numerous remains strewn about in most of the field. Some of these are signposted down rough tracks and include the temple of Apollo and the Praetorium, (the palace of the Roman governor) and a small ampitheatre. Excavations continue which may mean some parts are closed off but this still allows the opportunity to watch the archaeologists at work and see how much more of the site is being uncovered.

From Ayia Deka it is possible to get to Lendas on the coast by heading through Mitropolis.There is a paved road all the way and it is very important to find this road by turning right at Apesokari and avoiding the numerous dirt tracks or roads which peter out. Although these will eventually reach the coast, this will only be after an extremely long and stressful drive. Even the paved route is 26km (16 miles long) but the road is a good one.

**Lendas** is a tiny, quiet little village with a dusty car park as you enter. From here you can continue on foot by following the maze of alleys between and occasionally through the gardens of the residents and eventually reach a gently shelving beach.

Heading west beyond the cape, there are a couple of tavernas and a much longer, larger beach frequented by campers and nudists but big enough to accommodate those who do not wish to participate in either of these activities. It can be an exposed, windy place as Homer relates, describing the region as 'a smooth cliff at the verge of the territory of Gortyn, it stands sheer above the sea where the southwest wind drives a great surge towards the western headland'.

*Church in Pigaidakia*

**Leben,** close to the village of Lendas, was the ancient port of *Gortyn* and excavations have revealed the remains of a third-century temple to the god of healing, Asklepius. Various other remains suggest the place was known even then for its curative springs which were still visited until recently by those seeking the benefits of these waters.

Further west of Lendas, on a difficult dirt track which passes through a few small villages and beaches, is the harbour of Kali Limenes; a port in Roman times and the place where St Paul landed and wanted to spend the winter, calling it 'Fair Havens'. He was forced to move on and was later shipwrecked. The Venetians also had a port here for the harbour is the only safe year-round anchorage on the south coast, providing shelter from the winter storms which often strike this region. Nowadays, oil tankers unload at the two offshore islets but this does not mar the charms of its fine, sandy

*A view across the plain from Pigaidakia*

beach as much as might have been feared.

From Kali Limenes another dirt road runs north-west, reaching tarmac at Pigaidakia. It descends from the mountains to Pombia with magnificent views across the plain to Mires. The dirt road should not be attempted unless your vehicle is up to it and you are happy with travelling on such a surface.

Back on the plain are Mires and Timbaki, two towns of some size but little interest. In between them is the road to *Phaestos* (*Festos*), a couple of kilometres off the main road with extensive parking and served by frequent buses. The site is a short way uphill on a path leading to the tourist pavilion which sells various souvenirs and has a café serving drinks and snacks.

## Phaestos

*Phaestos* is the second largest Minoan palace and myths claim that this was the home of Rhadamanthys, one of Minos' younger brothers. As with *Knossos*, the palace has undergone several reconstructions. It was first built in 1900BC, destroyed in 1700BC, rebuilt and then finally destroyed in the great catastrophe of 1450BC. Much of the oldest palace has been uncovered which, although of great interest to the archaeologists, complicates the layout considerably. Furthermore, some of the site is fenced off and much of the East Wing of the palace has slipped down the hillside which can make the place perplexing and disappointing for the visitor. There is none of the reconstruction carried out at *Knossos* but, as with *Knossos*, the best idea is simply to wander round, picking up the significant features as you do so.

The modern entrance leads into the Upper Court which was possibly the market place and then there are stairs down into the West Court where the façades of the oldest palace and the newer one are both visible. Easily identifiable from here is the Theatral Area with its eight wide steps comprising the seating for the audience.

The way into the new palace is up the Grand Staircase, each stair is more than 13m (43ft) wide and is cut out of the rock, and then passing the storerooms into the Central Court. This is a 51.5m by 22.3m (169ft by 73ft) paved area and has, in its north-west corner, a stepped structure which could have been an altar or perhaps the point from where the athlete jumped onto the bull in the sport of bull leaping. The view from here is impressive; on clear days Mount Ida is visible, identifiable from the large dark mark on its face which is the Kamares Cave.

All around the court are the bases of pillars and, on the north side is the central doorway; the holes where the hinges were can still be seen on this. The stairs lead into the North Wing where the rooms of the King and Queen can be found. These are fenced off and have to be viewed by peering in from the side or, more effectively, by climbing up the stairs and looking in from above. As at *Knossos*, there is evidence of a sophisticated drainage system. Traces of the elegantly patterned floors remain but while there were substantial finds of other forms of art, no frescoes were found anywhere in the palace.

Slightly set back from the main buildings a number of storage chests were found, among them the *Phaestos* Disc. This is 16cm (6in) in diameter with script on both sides; each sign having been individually impressed to make 241 hieroglyphs arranged in a spiral. It has yet to be deciphered and is now in Iraklion Museum.

Much of the east wing has collapsed and fallen down the hillside leaving only a few small rooms and a Lustral basin. Nearby, a few storage pits and storerooms are visible.

Three kilometres (2miles) beyond *Phaestos*, taking the right hand

# Places of Interest South of Iraklion

**Arhanes**
A mountain village with three archaeological sites, one of which revealed the first evidence of human sacrifice by the Minoans.

**Vathipetro**
A remote Minoan villa where many tools and other implements were found.

**Mount Iouktas**
The legendary burial place of Zeus.

**Kastelli**
The biggest town in the region with all practical facilities.

**Ayia Meronas**
A small village with an underground chapel to St Meronas.

**Vrondisi Monastery**
A Venetian monastery, high up in the hills with fine examples of frescoes in the church.

**Valsamonero Monastery**
A ruined monastery with its church still standing, containing many fine frescoes.

**Kamares Cave**
A stiff climb from the village of Kamares, where the distinctive Kamares pottery was found.

**Gortyn**
An extensive Roman site where the famous law code can be seen.

**Lendas**
A little village near some fine, isolated beaches and an ancient temple.

**Phaestos**
The second of the Minoan palaces belonging to Minos' brother and where the famous *Phaestos* Disc was found.

**Ayia Triadha**
A Minoan villa with an unusual layout where many major finds were unearthed.

**Matala**
A beach with caves in the cliffs still famous from the hippy occupation in the 60s and 70s.

**Ayia Galini**
A fishing village that has grown into a holiday resort.

fork after the car park, is the villa of *Ayia Triadha* (*Aghia Triada*). The villa remains something of a mystery and there is no agreement on who might have lived here although possibly it was the summer residence of the kings of *Phaestos*. The layout is not the traditional one of buildings around a central court. Nonetheless, it certainly seems to have been an important place — there are rich finds of wall

Phaestos

paintings, delicately painted vases like the Chieftain's Cup and the Ayia Triadha sarcophagus, all of which are now in the Iraklion Museum.

It is important to note that the site closes at 3.30pm while *Phaestos* is open until 7pm in summer.

The site has been inhabited since the Neolithic period and the villa has been destroyed and rebuilt several times. The first excavations took place early this century and were carried out by the Italian school which has undertaken much of the work in this region.

The villa is L-shaped in form and, due to the confusion of the numerous layers of construction, the best first impression is gained from the higher ground looking down onto the building. In the corner of the 'L shape is the courtyard and slightly to the left of this area were the royal apartments. These consisted of several large halls with benches round the side and in one there is a platform which was probably a bed. The room in which the frescoes were found is also in this part of the palace.

The main section of the 'L' once contained the treasury and other storerooms but it seems the Myceneans occupied the site and built

*The sandy beach at Matala*

*Matala Bazaar*

royal apartments on top of these. Behind the spine of the 'L' is a ramp which the excavators called 'Rampa del Mare', a paved road they claimed might have led to the sea.

To the north of the site are the remains of the town which surrounded the villa, including a marketplace with shops arranged along one side. The tombs containing the sarcophagus were found in a cemetery beyond the town.

Also on the site is the little church of Ayios Yeoryios which dates from 1300 and contains frescoes of that period.

Returning from Ayia Triadha towards the *Phaestos* car park, one reaches a 'T' junction just before the car park. The road to the right leads to Pitsidia, Matala and the coast. The road descends the ridge on which *Phaestos* stands and flattens out amongst the olive groves. At the 'T' junction turn right for Matala. The road bypasses much of Pitsidia before climbing up the side of a hill towards Matala. At the top of the hill a rough track goes down to the sea at *Kommos* (*Komo*) where there is a good beach and the site is believed to have been the port for *Phaestos*. Excavations are continuing and have already revealed large numbers of Minoan houses and a Classical temple. These finds may be viewed through a fence.

There is a quiet, sandy and pebble beach here although flat slabs of rock occur in places which are slippery. Snorkellers may be able to see some of the town ruins which are now underwater. There is a taverna at the south end of the beach, above it on the cliffs there is a restaurant with a spectacular view which is well-used by local people; to reach it, take the next track off the Matala road.

**Matala** is most famous for its caves in the cliffs which have been inhabited since ancient times and more recently by a hippy community. The caves are now empty and visitors can climb up to them and look inside.

There is a pleasant, sandy beach here which can get crowded later in the day. Although modern development is forced by a narrow gap in the mountain to be on the landward side of the town, the main centre sits around its market place adjacent to the sea. Matala is well-equipped for dealing with the needs of the tourist and there is a range of shops including a bakery, large bookshop, post office and small supermarkets which open onto a bazaar. Those selling fruit offer to wash it on purchase. Among the various tavernas is one called Plaka which is right at the far end of the town and is recommended. To reach it, walk through the market place and down a short length of sea wall. This ends at the taverna where you can sit immediately above the sea, watching the countless fish and enjoying the splendid Matala sunsets.

Matala obviously owes its existence to tourism and those seeking peace and quiet will have to scramble over the rocks round to other more isolated beaches of which there are several close by. However, they are only accessible on foot. The best of these is known as Red Beach for the colour of its sand and is a 25 minute walk south of Matala. Parts of the beach are often taken over by nudists.

The other two resorts in the region are at **Kokkino Pirgos** and Ayia Galini. The former is a small town which is full of restaurants. It is a friendly place and, despite being as well-equipped for visitors as any resort, it does not have too great an influx of tourists. This makes it a curious, quiet village and the main evening excitement is the gathering of the locals on the quay before they go out fishing. There is a long beach; a mixture of grey sand and shingle which can be rather exposed on windy days.

**Ayia Galini** is a total contrast to Kokkino Pirgos; it is a small village which has most definitely become a big resort. Its narrow pedestrian streets which climb up the hill are crowded with restaurants and souvenir shops. Although very tourist-oriented, it still manages to retain a certain charm, especially out of season, by remaining for the most part within the fabric of the original fishing village.

There is a harbour at the bottom of the main street and a tiny patch of sand but the main beach is around the headland east of the town and is a long stretch of reasonable, coarse sand. On windy days, this can be less attractive but on the whole this is one of the better holiday resorts and easily accessible from the north coast for those simply wishing to spend the day here. To reach the main beach follow the easy path from the harbour. It is less crowded beyond the footbridge where a shallow river cuts across the beach.

*The holiday resort of Ayia Galini*

# 5
# *IRAKLION TO RETHIMNON*

T he journey between Iraklion and Rethimnon is a rapid one on the
new road and the coastline, which is steep and rocky, only allows
development in the few little coves found below it. The most interesting scenery can be found inland in the foothills and mountains of
the Ida Range. These are the highest peaks on the island and offer
many possibilities for strenuous climbs and even skiing in winter.

## Along the Coastal Road
Heading west out of Iraklion on the new road is not the prettiest drive
as it passes close to the port of Iraklion, the new industrial development and the oil storage tanks. The coastline soon becomes rocky and
the shore inacessible, partly because the road runs so close to the sea.
Only near Rogdia is there anything interesting to see; a ruined fort in
the cliffs above the road; it was built by the Genoese in 1206 and later
held by the Venetians and the Turks.

**Ayia Pelagia** is the first independent resort west of Iraklion and
is reached after 15km (9miles) by turning left off the main road and
then crossing back under it towards the sea. The drive down is steep
and ends in a rough car park. The actual main street of the town is
accessible only by turning off the descending road before the shore
but it is much simpler to stop in the car park and walk.

There is very little beach here because the restaurants are built so
close to the shore and the concrete walkway in front of them takes up
most of the rest of the sand. Therefore, if the sea is rough, it becomes
impossible to sit anywhere along the shore without getting wet.

The place claims to be an upmarket resort, a reputation which dates from the time when there were only a couple of luxury hotels here. Now the place is packed with apartments which have spawned a large modern supermarket, the like of which has never been seen on the island, and it is a crowded resort much like any other. The independent traveller is unlikely to have any luck finding a room, there are very few here and these are very expensive.

Seven kilometres (4miles) further west and a short distance inland is **Fodhele** which claims to be the birthplace of El Greco (1541-1611) although doubt has now been cast on this assertion. He was born in Crete but the exact location is far from clear. Despite Cretan attempts to associate him and his paintings with the island, the fact remains that he spent most of his life abroad in Spain.

The site where his house is supposed to have been is a 10 minute walk on a path running along the back of the village. A small modern building has been constructed here and although there are rumours of plans to open a museum, at the moment it is empty and locked. Much more interesting is the Byzantine church on the path below; although this is also usually locked the exterior is attractive, being of brown stone rather than the more usual, whitewashed walls.

The village itself is quite pretty and has a park in which there is a monument to the painter which was erected by a Spanish university. There are also a couple of churches and a small river. There are a few places to stay and a couple of cafés but these are decidedly primitive. The village is remarkably quiet during the day but extremely noisy at night when the farmers come in from the fields and the whole community seems to gather in the street to peel vegetables or pluck chickens.

A very bad track leads inland from Fodhele to the old Iraklion to Rethimnon road. Turning left here takes you to the village of Marathos which is known for its honey. The hives of these bees can be found in the mountains all around the area.

Back to the main road from Fodhele, heading towards Rethimnon, there is another stretch of rocky coastline until **Bali**, 22km (13$^1$/$_2$miles) away. This attractive cove is developing into a resort from its initial base around a luxury hotel. Earlier, it was a seaport for the Classical city of *Axos*, but no evidence remains of this role. It is not so much new as half-built and the road leading to it is extremely steep and bumpy. It is certainly quiet but not, as many would claim, 'away from it all'. Being caught between these two possibilities gives the place a curious atmosphere.

*Ayia Pelagia*

The resort encompasses three coves with rooms to rent and the odd shop on the cliffside above them. The first cove has a small beach and brown sand, the second seems to be taken over by the guests at the luxury hotel and the final bay might claim to be the centre of the village with harbour on one side and a strip of beach. Around the harbour are a few good value restaurants and a couple of souvenir shops along with places to hire boats.

A few kilometres beyond Bali is **Panormos**, a small village which seems much more 'Cretan' than Bali though perhaps this is because it is not solely a tourist resort. There are a few rooms to rent here, as well as a harbour and a beach but it remains a quiet and pleasant place. It was once an important commercial port for the Venetians who built a fortress here. It was sacked, firstly by Cretan rebels and later by Barbarossa. The Turks let it fall into disrepair and no trace of the village's history is visible today.

There are a few more beaches with large hotels beside them but little else until the approaches to Rethimnon. Here, the development is densely packed and stretches along the road for some considerable distance.

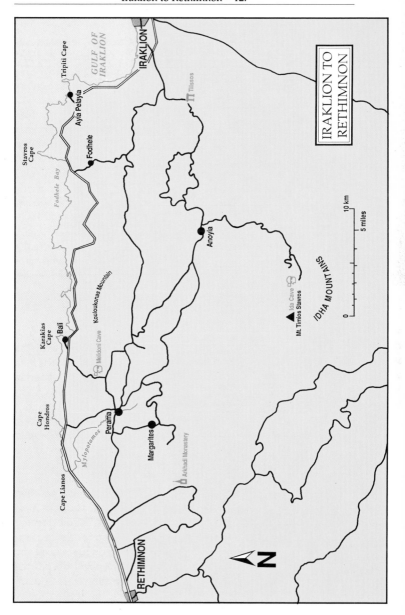

# Iraklion to Rethimnon Inland

Π   *Tilissos* is a major Minoan site in the hills, 14km (8$^1/_2$ miles) south-west of Iraklion. Although it does not rank with the palaces, consisting of three villas, it is still felt to be a site of some significance.

The villas are not easy to find; coming from Iraklion turn left as you enter the village; there is a tiny sign but only the eagle-eyed will spot it. Once in the village, the signs are better and the route doubles back down a narrow road. A free car park is advertised but there is a catch. The car park is actually a villager's back yard and, on pulling up, drivers are likely to be approached by a woman who offers to show you her weaving. The villas themselves are about 100m (330ft) beyond the 'car park'.

The site was first excavated early this century and the houses, labelled A,B and C, date mainly from the Late Minoan period 1600-1450BC. House A is the best-preserved and its ruins the most easily comprehensible. It was a two-storey building and the remains of the staircases are visible. There are also signs of the sophisticated Minoan drainage system with a flushing toilet probably in the house. Various storerooms are also discernible and in some cases the archaeologists have left the giant pithoi storage jars where they were found.

House B is the smallest and least well-preserved while in House C a complicated series of corridors can be seen along with the remains of a staircase. In one corner is a cistern dating from the Post Minoan period. This is evidence for the view that *Tilissos* was reoccupied after the Minoan collapse in 1450BC and later, in Classical times, it became one of the numerous city states on the island.

Heading towards the mountains, 6km (3$^1/_2$ miles) from *Tilissos*,
Π   is the fenced site of *Sklavokampos*, another villa. It is built in a simpler style than those at *Tilissos* but was extensively damaged during the war and there is not that much to see. The site is fenced off.

The road then climbs into the Psiloritis Mountains, the highest on the island. The village of **Anoyia**, which is at a height of 730m (2,394ft), is the next place of interest and is 10km (6miles) from *Tilissos*. The village is significant for several reasons, the most recent being its destruction by the Germans in retaliation for the kidnapping of General Kreipe, the German commander on the island. The story of the kidnap is told in the book *Ill Met by Moonlight*, despite the revelations of the amateurish nature of the operation.

Every building except the church was razed to the ground and so the village is completely modern but remains much visited by tourists, especially those on coach tours. The lower half of Anoyia is packed with shops selling items of weaving which range from rugs to blouses. Knitted dogs with curious facial features seem to be the regional speciality and, like all the goods, are marketed with some vigour. Many of the shops also serve as workshops and it is possible to watch the cloth been woven on large looms.

There is more to Anoyia than it might first appear and in the upper section of the village there are numerous cafés, a post office and a few shops, along with a large central square; this makes it one of the largest settlements in the region. It is also the starting point of the road which leads up to another cave which claims to be the birthplace of Zeus; the Ida Cave.

The road is tarmac most of the way, passing through the Nidha Plateau, one of several fertile plains on the island at high altitude which are used for summer grazing. The final approaches to the tourist pavilion are on a rougher road. Close by is the ski centre, as in winter the height of these mountains means the snow is extensive enough to allow for winter sports.

The cave is a good 15 minute walk beyond the pavilion and is not  that impressive in itself although important people have been coming here for centuries, most notably Pythagoras. The question of Zeus' association with the cave remains unresolved, with the Psychro Cave on the Lasithi Plain making a strong counterclaim to be his birthplace.

Excavations have been going on here for some time and continue today. The earliest finds date from 300BC but cover virtually all periods and include some impressive bronze shields, now in Iraklion Museum. Due to the excavations, the cave is closed to the public.

The tourist pavilion is the starting point for the numerous climbs in the region. The two best-known walks are that up to Mount Ida (Psiloritis) — at 2,456m (8,056ft), the highest mountain on the island — and that to the Kamares Cave on the south side of the mountain.

The climb to the summit of Ida should take about 8 hours there  and back. The path is reasonably well-marked by red splashes of paint on the rocks. The mountain can still be covered in snow in spring, and even later in the year it can be cold at the higher altitudes. There are some mountain springs on the way and a hut and a chapel at the summit. The peak is also accessible from the villages of the Amari Valley which lies to the west. Fourfouras is a well-used

*The Byzantine church at Fodhele basking in the evening sunshine*

starting point for the climb up to Ida while **Kamares** village is the best place to explore the southern side of the range as well as the Kamares Cave.

Near Anoyia is another small mountain village, **Axos**. The coaches tend to stop here before climbing up to Anoyia. There are good views out across the mountains from here and it has a pretty, little fifteenth-century church. There was an important ancient city state here, which, according to legend, was founded by Oaxos, one of Minos' grandsons. The city was also settled during the Roman and Byzantine periods but nothing really remains to be seen of these settlements.

Garazo, to the north-west, is a small village in similar style and just beyond it is the old Iraklion to Rethimnon road, the narrowness of which makes it clear how pressing the need must have been for the new one.

**Perama** is the only place of any size in the region and serves very much as a crossroads, with the routes for most of the interesting sites in the area passing through here. A wooden bridge crosses the

*Arkhadi Monastery*

Mylopotamus River and leads into the town. It is a large, busy place and full of locals rather than tourists. This is reflected, perhaps, in the fact that this is one of the few towns where all the fruit on sale is meticulously and visibly priced. All the facilities a visitor might need can be found on the main street and include a bank, bakery, café and a supermarket. If the driver can find a way round the double parking, which bedevils Perama, it can be an interesting and attractive place.

East out of Perama and back across the river are 4km ($2^1/_2$ miles) of bumpy road to **Melidoni** which presents one of the contrasts typical of the island; several modern factories juxtaposed with the distinctive mounds of neatly arranged branches of the charcoal burners.

The main interest at Melidoni is not the village but the cave which is a short distance away on a good road, well-signposted from the centre of the village. The cave is supposedly the home of Talus, a local giant who used to roam about the island throwing rocks at passing ships. Jason and his Argonauts were the most famous travellers to suffer from this bombardment. Talus came to a grisly end as, like most such creatures, he had a fatal flaw; his life depended on a bronze nail in his leg and when this was pulled out by the goddess Medea, he bled to death and Jason passed on safely.

Nowadays, the cave is a place of pilgrimage as the site in 1824 where nearly 400 villagers hid during a revolt against the Turks. The Turkish commander blocked the entrance to the cave and then asphyxiated all inside by lighting fires at the entrance. Robert Pashley, who travelled around the island 10 years later, found the cave strewn with bones and skulls. Many were deep inside the cave where the victims were overcome by fumes as they tried to flee. There is a shrine in the first cavern with an altar and some further caverns beyond, although a torch is necessary to see anything of this. There is also a small chapel on the site.

Further inland and 5km (3miles) south of Perama is **Margarites**, a small village known for its pottery. The potters can still be seen at work in the various workshops around the village and usually have a wide range of their goods for sale. However, there is little to see in the village apart from this.

Continuing into the mountains brings the visitor to the village of **Prines**, from where there is a path to the ancient site of *Eleutherna* (*Eleftherné*). This was a Dorian city state but the limited excavation that has been carried out has revealed very little of interest. The path passes the ruins of a tower from the Roman period, a small church and the remains of an acropolis. Some way beyond here and far from easy to find is a bridge dating from Classical Greek times; the best idea is to follow the stream. The bridge is about a 20 minute walk from the entrance to the site. A whole water sytem is visible on the east side of the settlement, including cisterns and a conduit.

The remaining place of interest in this region is one of the best-

# Places of Interest
## from Iraklion to Rethimnon

### *Coast*
**Ayia Pelayia**
A resort in a small cove down the cliffs with numerous apartments and restuarants.

**Fodhele**
The birthplace of El Greco, set in quiet countryside.

**Bali**
A growing holiday resort set around three coves.

### *Inland*
**Tilissos**
The site of three Minoan villas, showing the sophistication of Minoan drainage.

**Anoyia**
A mountain village destroyed by the Germans, now much visited for its woven goods.

**Ida Cave**
Claimed to be birthplace for Zeus, on the side of Crete's highest mountain.

**Melidoni Cave**
The site of a massacre of villagers sheltering here from the Turkish army.

**Arkhadi Monastery**
The central symbol of the Cretan Independence movement, a beautiful monastery whose defenders preferred to sacrifice themselves rather than surrender.

known; the **Arkhadi Monastery** some 15km (9 miles) inland off the old Rethimnon to Hania road. The drive is a pleasant one through olive groves and lush countryside although it does become quite steep as it nears the monastery.

The monastery stands very much as the symbol of the revolt against the Turks and the struggle for Cretan Independence. This is due to the events of 1866 when the monastery was besieged by the Turks. The Cretans inside refused to surrender. Then, when more troops arrived, seeing no hope of victory, the defenders inside waited until the building was stormed and blew up the gunpowder store. This action meant that not only were the Cretans killed but large numbers of the attackers as well. From this incident came the rallying call of the Independence movement; 'Freedom or Death'. On 9 November every year, this event is commemorated all over the island with games, fireworks and dancing.

The monastery dates mainly from the seventeenth century but

the much photographed and distinctive façade of the church was built in 1587 in an unusual mixture of extravagant and ornate styles. The remains of the store where the explosion took place are still visible and are marked by a plaque. There are various other rooms still standing around the courtyard including the refectory. All of these are somewhat stark and bear the scars of the battle.

The small museum contains three rooms with various relics of the period including priestly robes and other religious objects. The rogues gallery, with photographs of the Cretan rebellion's heroes, is unintentionally comic. There are pictures of rebels with astonishing moustaches who are wearing the traditional dress of baggy trousers and black headbands. The collection is completed by a chart detailing the Turkish advance on the monastery and various erratically labelled books and documents.

Various outbuildings stand in the grounds of the monastery. They include one where the visitor, on climbing up some steps to investigate, is confronted by several rows of neatly arranged skulls, apparently the traditional way of honouring the dead. The building is called 'The Sanctuary of the Dead' and contains the remains of thirteen victims of the Arkhadi battle. There is a tourist pavilion which sells souvenirs and drinks just beyond the car park.

# 6
# *RETHIMNON*

T he town of Rethimnon is a firm favourite with many visitors to Crete. It is situated halfway along the north coast of the island and easily accessible on the new road from both Iraklion and Hania; each about 1 hour's drive away. Furthermore, its position at one of the island's narrowest points means that the beaches at Ayia Galini and Plakias on the south coast are easily and quickly reached.

The city was probably inhabited in the Late Minoan period but very little excavation has been carried out to add to the find of Minoan tombs in a modern suburb. Aelian, a Roman writer, tells the story of a fisherman from the town, to whom Artemis revealed a cure for rabies. This anecdote and the discovery of coins issued by a town called *Rithymna* suggest that there was a Graeco-Roman settlement here but very little other evidence is available on this early period of Rethimnon's history.

As with all the major towns on the island, it is the Venetian period which has left the most extensive and visible legacy; a legacy which is perhaps the source of much of Rethimnon's charm.

The town was a centre of resistance against the Venetian occupation but this did not prevent it from playing a major role in the Cultural Renaissance that accompanied this period and many scholars and artists were resident in the city or making an impact in Venice.

It still claims to be the intellectual capital of the island, citing the work of Pandelis Prevelakis, who summed up the refined atmosphere of Rethimnon in his book *The Tale of a Town*. Many residents were somewhat disgruntled that this role was not acknowledged when only two departments of the University of Crete were built here.

The city suffered from repeated pirate raids during the sixteenth century. The infamous Barbarossa led an attack in 1538, during which the city was pillaged and many of the residents sold into slavery. A further raid in 1562, by Ali Pasha, prompted a radical reconsideration of the city's defences and the resulting decision to build the giant Fortezza which still dominates Rethimnon today.

The Turks began their full scale invasion of the island in 1645, besieging the three major cities of the north coast in turn. Hania capitulated quickly and the forces moved on to make a land and sea assault on Rethimnon. They captured the city easily and forced the population to shelter in the Fortezza. The siege of the fort lasted only 23 days although a cholera epidemic inside the fortress was as much responsible for the surrender as the strength of the attackers.

The Turks soon gained a strong grip on the city with the arrival of large numbers of settlers from the mainland. Many mosques were rapidly constructed and their minarets give Rethimnon its distinctive skyline. The Turks even converted the church in the heart of the Fortezza into a mosque, perhaps a sign of their dominance.

There was much ethnic violence between the Christian and Muslim communities. However, by the beginning of the nineteenth century, the Turkish population far outnumbered the Cretan residents and the city played only a minor role in the rebellions against the Turks of this period. The nearby mountains remained centres of resistance, most notably in the battle at Arkhadi Monastery which, as previously mentioned, has come to stand as the symbol of the Cretan struggle for Independence.

Rethimnon and the surrounding area were the scene of heavy fighting during the Battle of Crete as the town was one of the central objectives of the first German airborne assault. The attack was beaten off by a combination of Australian and Cretan resistance forces but the town soon fell when the Allies decided to evacuate the island.

The town is the third largest on the island but only has a population of 20,000. It lacks the extensive concrete sprawl of modern Hania or Iraklion and this makes it a relatively peaceful place to stay or visit.

This is not to say that it is a quiet seaside town. Through traffic still thunders across the centre of town from the main coast road with its usual impatience and cacophany of hooting. Eventually, a bypass should help resolve this problem. The approaches to Rethimnon, both from the east and the west, are not particularly attractive, distinguished only by the lines of hotels and holiday apartments. Many of these are still under construction and only add to the noisy, dusty atmosphere.

However, the heart of the city manages to retain a certain dignity and composure especially around the harbour and along the sea front, where it is possible to park. It is advisable to avoid the many narrow streets of the old town when driving. These are better explored on foot when the Venetian doorways and Turkish fountains, which remain in all corners of the city, can be appreciated.

Rethimnon has plenty of holiday accomodation; the apartments and hotels are strung along the approach roads to the city, while the cheaper rooms are closer to the centre, behind the harbour and below the Fortezza.

One of the major features of eating out in Rethimnon is the sheer abundance of restaurants. The whole of the harbour area is taken over by the tables of the various fish restaurants fully exploiting their romantic setting. Along the sea front are the more overtly tourist-oriented cafés with their eager waiters approaching passers-by in multi-lingual attempts to lure them into their particular establishments.

All other services can be found around the town; there are numerous banks, telephone and post offices and large supermarkets near the apartment blocks. The tourist office is just behind the beach.

There are two bus stations with buses for Hania and Iraklion leaving from Iroon Square, a short distance back from the beach. Buses serving the south of the island leave from Dimokratias Street; turn off Kountouriotou opposite the town hall.

The **Fortezza** claims to be the 'largest ever built' and its size is certainly impressive. It was constructed in response to repeated pirate raids against the city. Building began in 1573, on the site of a Byzantine fortress, starting with the defensive sea walls. A second phase then followed to allow all the necessary installations inside the fortress to sustain the population should they need to shelter here. These included St Nicholas Cathedral, barracks, a hospital and storerooms. However, when the Turkish invasion came, the defenders only managed to resist for 23 days and, on being captured, many were sold as slaves in the Istanbul market.

The entrance to the fort can be found by either scrambling up a dirt path from the coast road which runs around it, or approaching it from the old town. Its size makes it easy to find and wandering

*The Fortezza, Rethimnon*

*The castle mosque, Rethimnon*

around the town side of the walls will eventually reveal the way in.

The coast road, which begins beyond the harbour and rounds the point with the sea on one side and the huge walls on the other, is a good way to gain an impression of the extent of the structure, as well as being a pleasant walk. To reach the fort from the coast, simply turn left at the first opportunity beyond the walls (Melissinou Street) and bear left again about 600m (660yd) later as one nears the town. The entrance is at the top of a cobbled street.

Once inside, it is perhaps best to follow the walls again for the wonderful views they offer of the city and its minarets, the mountains beyond and the harbour below.

Most of the structures within the grounds, in the much overgrown centre, are now in ruins and not easily identifiable but include the officers' quarters and underground gunpowder and weapon stores. The square mosque with its distinctive dome is the best-preserved building and it is possible to peer inside and to examine its mosaic patterned ceiling. Near the mosque is the small church of St Catherine which still seems to be in use. At the entrance to the fort is a café which sells postcards and drinks which tend to be expensive.

✳ Perhaps the most picturesque area of the town is the **Venetian harbour**, with the old houses on its quay now converted to restaurants. An old lighthouse stands at the end of the curving harbour wall and is illuminated at night. The restaurants themselves add considerably to the atmosphere with their colourful displays of fish and fruit. It is interesting to see how the mood of the area changes throughout the day. In the early morning everything is scrubbed clean, the tables laid and new displays constructed in the cold cabinets. In the evening, when the atmospheric low lights are reflected in the water and the waiters bustle back and forth, it seems a different place.

After the harbour, the town presents a total contrast. The long sea front promenade is much more overt in its tempting of the tourists, with the ubiquitous souvenir shops and plethora of cafés and restaurants stretching along its length.

Behind all this is yet another different environment; that of the Old Town with its narrow busy streets where the fashionable clothes shops are juxtaposed with ancient old men in traditional dress working leather or metal.

🏛 The **Archaeological Museum** is on the road heading into the Old Town between the harbour and the seafront. It is housed in the Venetian Loggia which was a meeting hall for the nobility of the time. The Turks converted it to a mosque and the remains of a minaret are still visible at the back of the building. At the time of writing the museum is closed for renovation and there is no indication of when or if it will reopen. Should it do so, it is worth visiting for its miscellaneous collection of local finds from the Minoan tombs found in the Mastaba district of the city, as well as bits and pieces of Graeco-Roman art found in the area and a large number of coins.

✳ The road continues away from the sea to the **Arimondi Fountain**. This is quite easy to miss as it is hidden by the cafés which surround it and is built into one of them. It was built in 1623 and water was channelled through the mouths of the three lions.

Many of the houses in this area are extremely old, with Venetian façades and doorways visible in almost every street. Somehow, their crumbling state does not seem to detract from their charm but rather adds to the attraction of the area.

🕌 Visible from the fountain is the **Nerantzes Djani** minaret, attached to a Venetian church which was built in 1227. The structure was converted to a mosque on Turkish occupation and the minaret added.

*A modern sculpture of dolphins on the breakwater, Rethimnon*

It is possible to climb the minaret and the views from the top are magnificent. However, there is no regulation of ascent or descent and passing the crowds coming the other way on a dark, narrow spiral stairway is somewhat dangerous.

Near the minaret is **Odhos Ethnikis Antistaseos**, the heart of the market area. The Venetian **church of San Fransisco** is on the right hand side of this road, now restored and used as a concert hall. Despite the number of tourists, this part of town has genuinely local

The Venetian harbour and old lighthouse,
Rethimnon

*A view over Rethimnon from the Fortezza*

*The Arimondi Fountain is now sur-rounded by contrasting modern buildings*

atmosphere. Produce of all kinds is colourfully displayed outside the shops and is carried off in bulging bags by Cretan women.

The street meets the main road and the modern city at **Porta Guora**, a gateway in the old Venetian city walls which is the only visible reminder of these installations.

The road now enters the **Plateia Tessaron Martyron**; a square dominated by the modern church of that name. It is named after four brothers martyred in 1824 by the Turks and is one of several large, more recent churches in the city that the visitor is bound to come across while exploring Rethimnon. Also visible from the square is another minaret with neither name nor mosque.

Across the road are more market stalls selling fruit and vegetables brought in from the villages and on the other side of the main south coast route are the **Public Gardens**. Once a Turkish cemetery, they now contain busts of various Cretan notables. The park is a reasonably quiet, if dusty place.

Towards the end of July, the annual wine festival is held here in the gardens. There is folk dancing, music, food and, of course, plentiful wine; visitors take their own drinking vessel and fill it from the barrels. It is also possible to buy a glass or a jug while you are there. It attracts local residents as well as the tourists and is certainly worth a visit if one is in the town during this period.

Beyond the Tessaron Martyron Church is Kountouriotou; one of the city's main roads, on which the OTE (telephone office) and post office can be found. This office only has one cabin for international calls and there is a much better office, which caters much more for holidaymakers, at the far end of the beach.

To the south of Kountouriotou, in the modern part of town, is another mosque called **Kara Pasha**. It was converted from a Venetian monastery and retains its dome and minaret.

Back near the seafront is Odhos Victor Ougo; Victor Hugo gave his support to the Cretans fighting for independence from the Turks and was rewarded by having this street named after him. A short distance along this street is the domed Veli Pasha Mosque with a rather scruffy garden in front. It is closed to the public.

It is perhaps the town as a whole rather than individual monuments which make Rethimnon such an attractive place. It is not yet overwhelmed by tourists nor pre-packaged for them but rather seems to proceed, unperturbed, with the real business of the day.

Rethimnon has a futher asset in its beach which is right in the

# Places of Interest in Rethimnon

**Fortezza**
The huge Venetian fortress built to keep out the Turks. It has massive walls and wonderful views of the city.

**Harbour**
Picturesque Venetian harbour with an old lighthouse and fish restaurants around the quay.

**Arimondi Fountain**
A Venetian fountain with three lions' heads, it is surrounded by pleasant cafés.

**Nerantzes Djani Minaret**
Slender minaret; a relic of the Turkish occupation. Visitors can climb its spiral steps.

**Porta Guora**
The only surviving remains of the Venetian city walls, an arched gateway.

**Plateia Tessaron Martyron**
The main square, with a large modern church at one end, a daily market and the Public Gardens.

**Beach**
Shallow sea and clean sand at the centre of the town with a promenade behind.

centre of the town and is surprisingly clean and sandy. Parasols and beds are available for hire and there are a couple of bars on the beach itself. Between the harbour and the breakwater, the sea is virtually enclosed and is very calm and shallow. Walking up to the harbour wall, another beach is revealed beyond it. This is often crowded with the residents of the hotels and apartments which spread along this stretch of coast. The sea is usually rougher here but there are more facilities for water sports.

On the breakwater, there is an interesting modern sculpture with ✳ two dolphins entwined. This is the town symbol and originates from the ancient coins minted by the ancient city of *Rithymna*.

At the western side of the town the shore is very rocky and, as the road runs very close to the sea, there is no beach until well out of town.

*Typical narrow street in Rethimnon*

# 7
# SOUTH OF RETHIMNON

Rethimnon lies at one of the narrowest parts of the island and therefore allows easy access to the south coast. This region remains undeveloped because the mountains make many parts difficult to reach. In areas like the Amari Valley the visitor is sure to encounter a slower pace of life and traditions untouched by time. There is history here but it is quieter and less flamboyant than in other regions.

There are two major routes across the island in this region, both of which finish at the south coast holiday resort of Ayia Galini. The first road leaves from the suburbs just east of Rethimnon and is a quieter, slower road than the direct route from the centre of town.

## The Amari Valley

This first route leads through the Amari Valley, sees few tourists and makes a particularly pleasant excursion. The early part of the drive is through low hills and lush vegetation. Then, as the road begins to climb, there are good views back down towards the coast and several interesting rock formations in the distance.

The pass at Apostoli leads into the valley itself and a good road allows the driver to take either a clockwise or an anti-clockwise route to the south coast, or even a leisurely circuit around the whole region. The valley has a long and violent history and most of the villages on its western side are modern, the original ones having been destroyed by the Germans in reprisal for the actions of the resistance. At their centre is, invariably, a war memorial commemorating the region's role and sacrifice in the conflict.

While few of the villages have sites of specific interest, their unspoiled communities give a unique insight into village life and the traditional farming methods still used today. The region seems to have a particularly high donkey population, and it retains a rustic charm.

Travelling in a clockwise circuit, the first village of interest is **Thronos**, 1km ($^1/_2$ mile) off the main road. In the centre is an old church which may date back to the fourth century; beside it the remains of a mosaic are visible through the dust. Inside are frescoes from the early fourteenth century.

The village is built on the site of the Classical city of *Sibyrita* (*Syvrita*) which was important enough to mint its own coins. The acropolis of this city is visible above the settlement. It is reached by a path leading up the slope opposite the church which then passes along a stretch of ancient city wall. Not much else has been excavated although there are good views across the valley from the site.

Beyond Thronos is the real heart of the valley which seems to support every kind of vegetation from cacti to olive trees, with the odd palm as well. At the Moni Asomaton; once a rich monastery now an agricultural school, is the road to Amari itself. This is a short pleasant drive of 5km (3miles) on a narrow road with a few steep turns. Just outside the village is the church of Ayia Anni, famous for its frescoes which have a date of 1225 marked on them by the artist. Unfortunately, they are not very well-preserved. The church is down a track opposite the police station.

The village of **Amari** is a maze of alleys through the whitewashed houses and goatsheds. It is overlooked by a Venetian clocktower which, although visible from every street, is surprisingly difficult to find. The access is through the grounds of the church, round the back and up some steps to join a dusty path. The tower is open and the whole eastern side of the valley is visible from the top. There is a café and a phone office in the village but very little else.

By continuing round the valley, the visitor reaches **Vizari**. To the west, on a bad track, are the remains of a Roman town and a very early Christian church dating from the eighth century which reflects the importance of the region at that time. The site is overgrown and the ruins can be hard to identify.

Beyond here is **Fourfouras**, another pretty little village from where walkers head into the Psiloritis Mountains. Kouratis (Kouroutes) and Nithavri stand at the southern end of the valley from

where the road turns across to Ayios Ioannis. Here a bridge crosses
the river and there are good views of the mountains and the coast
below. This is the point where those wishing to head for Ayia Galini
should turn south.

Coming up the other side of the valley, just beyond Kardaki, is the
abandoned monastery of Ayios Ioannis Theologos. These ruins are
still impressive and contain some rapidly fading frescoes, the earliest
of which dates from the thirteenth century.

**Yerakari** is a village typical of the area; burned down by the
Germans and only rebuilt after the war. **Meronas**, a little further
along the road, escaped such destruction and has a Venetian church
in a distinctive orange/pink colour with frescoes from the fourteenth
century. Just opposite is a mountain spring and a little further into
the village is a shady park with a war memorial.

# Across the Island Via Spili

The second route across the island leaves Rethimnon at the Public
Gardens and is not signposted. The road climbs steeply out of the city
and there are good views back across its distinctive skyline.

This road passes through very few villages and the only site of
interest is in the early part of the drive. This is the Minoan cemetery
at Armeni, signposted on the right. The cemetery dates from the Late
Minoan period. A number of sarcophagi were discovered in tombs
cut out of the rock along with various weapons and ornaments which
are all now displayed in Iraklion Museum.

Although this road is tarmac all the way and reasonably wide, it
is plagued by the peculiar Cretan phenomenon of unfinished and
abandoned roadworks. These only add to the hazard of subsidence
at the edge of the road and mean as much care is required here as on
the more minor mountain routes.

Twenty-six kilometres (16 miles) from Rethimnon is the village of
**Spili**; a particularly verdant place, still relatively quiet despite being
on the tourist coach trail and boasting a hotel and a bank as well as
shops and cafés. It is famous for its mountain springs and the water
from these emerges through the mouths of nineteen stone lions into
a very long trough. Six more conventional water pipes beyond the
lions are still used by local women as a source of water. Look for this
feature above a bend in the road in the middle of the village.

A climb up the alleys into the real village offers insights into the
mountain life, with black-clad women sitting outside doing their

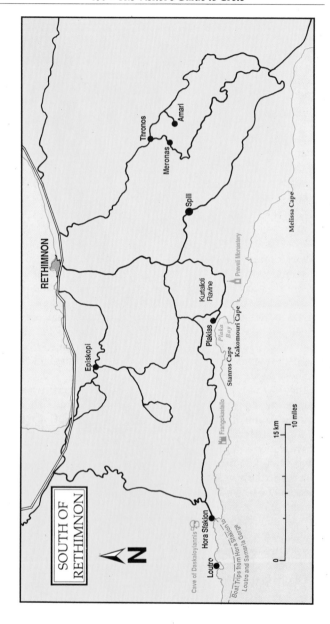

*The ancient churches at Thronos and Amari*

crochet or goats poking about in gardens. It all seems a different world even from the main road 100m (330ft) below.

This main road continues swiftly and uneventfully down to Ayia Galini. There are marvellous views and several little villages en route which show Crete at its most rural with people riding on donkeys and carrying on their lives regardless of tourists.

North of Spili is a turning which heads west through the Kurtaliko (Kurtalioti) Ravine, one of the many impressive gorges on the island. In summer it is a dry river bed with steep rock faces on either side. This is the route to the Preveli Monastery which is well-signposted all the way. Just before the final turning up to the monastery are the remains of an arched bridge over the Megapotamos River, one of only five on the island which does not dry up in summer. The lush vegetation and sound of rushing water make this an attractive and unique place.

Just beyond here is a left turn up to Preveli. The road is fairly steep and potholed. On the left is the ruined monastery of Ayios Ioannis, from where the monks moved to the current building in the seventeenth century. It is a curious place, still impressive from a distance but further exploration is difficult as it seems to have been taken over by goats and goatherd.

The **Preveli Monastery** is at the far end of this road. It is famous for its role in the evacuation of Allied soldiers after the Battle of Crete who were taken off the island by submarine from the nearby beach after being sheltered here. A plaque in the courtyard commemorates this event and thanks the monastery for its help. The monks were active in earlier rebellions against the Turks when they supplied rebel ships. The most famous of these was the Arkadi which made frequent visits to the island during 1866 to deliver guns to the rebels.

Most of the monastery dates only from the nineteenth century although there is a fountain in the grounds which is 100 years older. Its setting, high above the Libyan Sea, is particularly spectacular.

Back down the road, a path across the red soil to the cliff edge is visible. This leads to the stunning **Preveli Beach** with its palms and lagoon; a true paradise setting. Some cars do risk this track but it seems foolhardy to do so and much better to park and walk. It takes 10 minutes to the cliff edge from where there are a maze of paths leading down to the sea. Despite the arrows painted on the rocks, the route is not always obvious. There follows a good 10 minutes of steep descent for which good shoes and a reasonable amount of agility are necessary. All the way down there are tantalising glimpses of the beach below and it really is worth the exertions required to reach it.

There is another route to the beach which involves following the track across the river at the arched bridge before one even turns off to the monastery. This leads to a taverna and from here there is a scramble round to the beach and this too, is a far from easy walk.

The place consists of a strip of sand behind which the river curves round to the sea, resembling a tropical lagoon. In summer it is easy to wade upstream surrounded by palms, oleanders and waterfalls as the gorge narrows making a beautiful and unusual scene.

The beach and the sea are superb. The place is often frequented by nudists and by boats bringing visitors in for day trips. The boats tie up on the shore, hampering swimming and leaving an oily film on the surface of the, otherwise clear, water. However, in all other respects, the place remains an unspoiled idyll for the moment.

Rejoining the road westward, it is a short drive to **Plakias**, a growing resort with plenty of rooms and restaurants. Despite this, it is still a small village consisting only of the main street along the sea front and a couple of tracks inland. The beach here is the main attraction as it stretches right around the bay in a fine, sandy swathe.

There are other beaches in the vicinity, in the coves east of the village. The most popular of these is **Danoni** (Damnoni) which has a taverna and lighter coloured sand than that at Plakias but can be crowded. There are a few more secluded coves beyond it, one of which is taken over by nudists.

If you are retracing your steps from here, there is an alternative road to the Kurtaliko Ravine. Turn left off the road to the latter and climb up the adjacent gorge. It is equally spectacular and emerges at the top with pleasant views across to Asomatos and the surrounding hills. Follow this through the village to the main Rethimnon to Ayia Galini road.

The main road west out of Plakias climbs steeply and offers great views of the bay below, especially from the villages of Mirthios and Sellia. This road goes west all the way to Hora Sfakion and is a very quiet drive, offering spectacular scenery virtually all the way.

Rodakino is the biggest place in the area but there is very little to see and it is distinguished more by the appalling section of road which passes through it than anything else. Just beyond Rodakino, the paved road stops and it is 3km (2 miles) to the next tarmac section. However, the dirt track is not too bad.

*Preveli Monastery*

*Preveli Bay (right)*

Soon after regaining the tarmac section, the road begins to descend to the coastal plain with the impressive silhouette of **Frangokastello** coming into view. This is 3km (2miles) down a straight, newly paved road. The castle was built in 1371 by the Venetians in order to subdue the region and to deter pirate raids. The Turks then took it over, interrupted for a brief period when Cretan rebels, led by Dalianis, fought a battle here and were easily defeated and killed.

This was a typical example of Cretan defiance obscuring sensible military strategy; the rebellion would have had much more success had the rebels fought from the mountains. Instead of this, they stood and tried to defend a hopeless position and were massacred. The local legend has it that on the anniversary of this event every year, at dawn, the ghosts of this defeated army return. These spectres are called *dhrousoulites* or 'dew shadows'. The legend also lives on in folk songs, Daliani being the archetypal *palikari*, a hero who died for his cause.

The castle is at its most impressive from a distance. There is nothing left inside and it is overgrown and often strewn with rubbish. In front of the fort is a long stretch of white sand with sea that remains shallow even 100m (330ft) from the shore. It is obviously not ideal for serious swimming but is a particularly tranquil place and is very safe for children.

There are a couple of tavernas near the castle and some development has taken place on the road to the west. However, this remains very low key, consisting of a few rooms and unofficial camping. For other facilities, the visitor has to head inland to one of the villages although none of these are sizeable places.

The main road climbs back into the hills and, 12km ($7^1/_2$ miles) later, arrives at **Hora Sfakion**; a tiny village squashed in a little cove between the mountains. It has a savage history, being at the centre of the notoriously lawless Sfakia region and still retains a strong sense of tradition and pride in its habits of rebellion and banditry. The village has a long history dating from the sixteenth century, when it was the major south coast town, a fact which seems barely believable given the size of the place today. Its other incredible claim is that it contains 100 churches; just finding the space for all these, never mind the level of piety, would seem to be the main problem.

Little of this is evident to visitors today, most of whom only stay the time it takes to get off a boat from the base of the Samaria Gorge

# Places of Interest South of Rethimnon

**Amari Valley**
One route across the island passes through this rural region full of pretty mountain villages including:

*Thronos*
Has a very old church and some remains of an ancient city.

*Amari*
Its Venetian clock tower has a fine view from the top.

*Meronas*
Venetian church with fourteenth-century frescoes.

**Spili**
This is an attractive mountain village, famous for its springs in the form of nineteen lions.

**Preveli**
*Preveli Monastery*
A nineteenth-century monastery which has a tradition of helping rebels, most recently Allied soldiers during their evacuation in 1941.

*Preveli Beach*
A real paradise where the river meets the sea in a peaceful, palm-lined lagoon.

**Plakias**
A small village which is growing into a resort with a fine beach stretching around the bay. Still quiet despite all the development.

**Frangokastello**
An eerie silhouette in the distance marks this Venetian castle. All its outer walls are still standing but it is a shell inside. By a beautiful beach.

**Hora Sfakion**
The disembarkation point for weary gorge walkers, a quiet little village squeezed in on this rugged coast.

**Loutro**
A village only accessible by boat from Hora Sfakion or by energetic walkers. Rapidly becoming a tourist centre but still very quiet.

**Askifou**
The central village of the plain, halfway across the island. A quiet rural area although once a battlefield.

and climb onto a coach. After the boats have stopped running, the village is really very quiet, with little to do except stroll past its restaurants or sit on the tiny beach. It is literally in the middle of nowhere but its isolation was a useful factor in the evacuation of large numbers of Allied troops from the village after their retreat in 1941. These events are commemorated by a war memorial above the beach.

*Visitors to Hora Sfakion leaving the ferry*

*Hora Sfakion*

Boats go from here to Ayia Roumeli at the foot of the Samaria Gorge, stopping at the village of Loutro on the way. The boat trip is worthwhile even if the gorge is ignored, simply for the view it offers of this otherwise inaccessible coastline. The mountains come straight down to the sea, presenting a towering and incredibly barren aspect.

**Loutro** is accessible only on foot or by boat. In recent years it has made its isolation a virtue and some holiday companies now offer Loutro as a destination to get away from it all. In fact, large numbers of tourists seem to spend the night here and it can be quite crowded. The more appearances the village makes in the brochures the more rash the promises of getting off the beaten track will prove to be.

This area is known for its storms and numerous illustrious travellers have been shipwrecked in the surrounding seas. Loutro itself is the only safe year-round anchorage on the south coast. The whole area with its bleak, bare mountains can seem eerie and threatening as, even in the summer, the mist swirls round the summits.

Out of Hora Sfakion is a road to the west which is very steep and leads to **Anopoli**. This remote mountain village was the home of

Daskaloyiannis, the famous Sfakian rebel who came to a grisly end, being skinned alive in Iraklion. His exploits are recorded in *The Song of Daskaloyiannis*; a dramatic rendering of the revolt which tells of his ill treatment at the hands of the Turks and his Russian backers who failed him. Numerous caves in the area are also associated with him.

Anopoli was a prosperous Roman and Byzantine town with a large population but very little evidence remains of this former role today. The actual site is a good 20 minute walk west of the village by the Ayia Ekaterini Church. Some remains of the walls are all that can be made out. The ancient city had its port at *Phoenix*, now the modern village of Loutro. There is a well-worn path which follows the ancient route down to the coast. The descent is extremely steep but reasonably rapid.

From Anopoli there are other walks possible, including the 8 hour climb to Pahnes. At 2,452m (8,042ft), this is the highest mountain in the Levka Ori.

The only tarred road from Anopoli leads to **Aradena**, 2km (1 mile) away. This is a settlement which lies on the far side of the Aradena Gorge, one of the most spectacular on the island. The village is almost deserted but there is an impressive Byzantine church perched on the edge of the ravine. It is accessible either by descending into the gorge or taking the new bridge which now spans it. Although the church dates from the fourteenth century, it is thought to be built on the site of a much earlier Christian basilica. There are some early frescoes inside.

Beyond Aradena, the road is really too rough for cars and leads to the village of **Ayios Ioannis**, a larger place with two Byzantine churches and some interesting caves. The village was the site of yet another defiant act of resistance by locals, this time against the Egyptians who were reinforcing Turkish troops. As ever, the Cretan rebels, heavily outnumbered, died heroes.

There are numerous possibilities for long-distance walks between Hora Sfakion and Ayia Roumeli although these should be regarded as major expeditions and care should be taken to investigate boat connections before setting out. The path from Hora Sfakion to Loutro is the most widely used and follows the coast closely, allowing stops at beaches. The walk takes about 2 hours.

From Loutro to Ayia Roumeli is a much more difficult walk, being much longer and not well-marked. About three-quarters of the way along the walk is the small chapel of Ayios Pavlos where St Paul is supposed to have landed and carried out a few baptisms in the nearby stream. Ayia Roumeli is about 1 hour from here.

Travelling back across the island from Hora Sfakion is relatively quick and easy. The road, though new, is steep and narrow and there is a steady stream of coaches heading to and fro, collecting people from the gorge. Care should be taken, as the drivers are notoriously reckless.

The road climbs steeply out of the village and in the early morning the mountains are covered in mist as they loom over the sea. The road then passes through the Imbros Ravine, with high mountainous landscapes, barren save for the ubiquitous and incongruous purple heather. Because of the position of the road, the views of the ravine itself are disappointing.

At the other end of the ravine is the surprisingly green, flat Plain of Askifou which lies at a height of 730m (2,394ft). Askifou is also the name of the biggest village in the area which seems to consist only of houses; like so many of these mountain villages, there are no shops.

The plain itself was the site of a battle fought between rebels and the Turks in 1821. For once, the rebels won and a whole heroic folklore developed around the victory which is still evident in the songs today. They won the battle but lost the war which only provided further material for the song writers. There are ruins of a Turkish fort at the head of the plain.

There are few other villages on the road as it re-enters a rather barren landscape before descending to Vrisses and the main north coast highway described in the next chapter.

*Frangokastello*

*Ayia Roumeli*

*Loutro*

# 8

# *RETHIMNON TO THE AKROTIRI PENINSULA*

T he drive from Rethimnon to Hania is not the most memorable on the island, passing through low hills and an undistinguished, rocky coast. It does, however, contain the island's only natural lake and the approaches to Souda Bay, with the views across to the Akrotiri Peninsula, compensate for any dullness encountered earlier on the road.

There are two main roads running west from Rethimnon; the old and the new. The latter keeps close to the coast, the former heads inland and neither have an enormous number of places worth stopping for on the route, especially in the first few kilometres.

About 6km (4miles) from Rethimnon, just off the new road, is **Gerani** (Yerani) where there is a cave. It was discovered when the new road was being built, and contained Neolilthic remains. It is not open to the public, but the coast here is accessible and there is a good, if rocky beach.

The old road passes through several small villages until it reaches Episkopi, a more sizeable place from where a detour can be made up to **Agiroupoli** (Argyroupoli) which is built on the ancient city of *Lappa*. Some make the unlikely claim that it was founded by Agamemnon. The city state was extremely powerful and held out against the Romans long after the rest of the island had fallen. It was eventually captured and settled by the invaders. Today it is more famous for its springs which run into cisterns and water mills below the village.

Further into the mountains is **Asigonia**, a well-known centre for ✳ Cretan folklore and culture. It was also the home of George Psychou-dakis, the author of *Cretan Runner*; an account of the resistance movement on the island and local participation in it.

One of the roads west from Episkopi leads to the only natural lake on the island; Lake Kournas. Covering 160 acres, it is a sizeable expanse of water, although in dry summers its levels do go down considerably. It is surrounded by mountains and so appears in a bowl-shaped setting. The lake, with its ever-changing shades of blue and green in the shadows of the mountains, is a particularly attrac-tive place. There are numerous stories of the ghosts of drowned maidens and other mysterious phenomena appearing in the waters.

There are plenty of secluded places around the shore to picnic or there are tavernas on the track above. Depending on the level of the lake, it may be possible to walk some of the way around it or indulge in the distinctly un-Mediterranean pursuit of feeding the ducks. Visitors might also like to take the opportunity of swimming in freshwater or hiring a pedalo.

From here there is a road down to the coast and **Georgioupolis** which lies at the western end of a very long beach. The town, such as it is, stands around a central square which also serves as the car park. There are a few cafés in or near the square and some tracks which lead down to the beach. On one of these there is a small supermarket.

The nearby river runs down into the sea, which is not always especially clean. In fact, the damp, marshy ground led to the town's reputation for being one of the unhealthiest places on the island. Before the war, it had a high incidence of malaria among its popula-tion but this problem has long been eradicated.

On the approaches to the shore there seems to be nothing but building work which only adds to the dusty atmosphere. The beach itself is long and sandy. There is a causeway running out to a small chapel and in the harbour a rusting hulk of some kind of troop transport ship.

The town is named after Prince George of Greece who was High Commissioner of the island in the inter-regnum between independ-ence and *Enosis* (union with Greece). When the sun shines it is a pleasant place but lacks all the facilities of a major resort although it does have a widely advertised cinema. Films are subtitled rather than dubbed and the experience of open-air cinema is one which visitors should try if they have the opportunity.

All the main roads in the area seem to head for **Vrisses** (Vrises). This has tree-lined streets and a river. Unfortunately, the latter is dry most of the year and the former dusty and rubbish-strewn. However, by the river there is a monument to Cretan independence, along with a number of restaurants and cafés.

Drivers should be aware that Vrisses is the main crossroads of the region and roads head out of the village in all directions. They should particularly note the potential for confusion with signs both to the old and new Rethimnon to Hania roads.

*The bay at Almyrida*

North of Vrisses it is possible to explore the area around Vamos and the Drapanos Cape which is a very distinctive region and quite different to that which has preceded it. The landscape is flat and the roads very quiet and narrow. The villages are tiny, pleasant and peaceful. It is possible to get right out to the cape although there are few signposts in the region and drivers should be careful not to end up in any of the military areas.

At the far tip of the peninsula, on its western side, are the small villages of Kokkino Horio and Plaka. They both boast about the respective roles they played in the film *Zorba the Greek*. Coming down to the sea from these villages, which are perched in the cliffs, there are

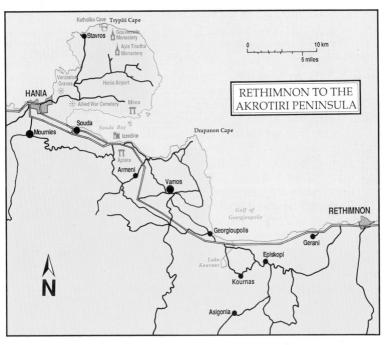

*The Allied War Cemetery near Souda*

good views across **Souda Bay**. This is one of the finest deep water anchorages in the Mediterranean and is of strategic importance to NATO. It was even more crucial during World War II; many British ships were sunk here under aerial bombardment from the Germans in 1941. An inlet 15km (9 miles) long and in parts 16km (10 miles) wide, the bay now contains a NATO base as well as that of the Greek Navy and the bars in Hania are kept going in the off season by visiting sailors.

On the coast, the first reasonable beach is **Almyrida**, a fairly long stretch of sand with tavernas at one end. However, a large proportion of the water contains underwater rocks which extend out quite far, making it difficult to find somwhere to swim. There is a small area facing the clear water but this inevitably gets rather crowded, especially at weekends.

In terms of beaches, **Kalives**, a short way along the coast, seems a much better prospect. It is a large place but has very little tourism and a long, pleasant beach which is seldom crowded.

On a hill above the road towards Hania is **Izzedine**, once a Turkish fort and now a prison. Nearby is the ancient site of *Aptera*. Reaching the site is not easy; it means heading inland from the main road to Kalami and the prison beyond. The whole area is surrounded by the various military installations of the base at Souda and there are many areas where photography is not allowed.

Beyond the prison are the ruins of the Turkish fort and then the site of *Aptera*. This was a powerful city state, commanding this strategic position overlooking the bay. *Aptera* means wingless and is thought to derive from the myth of a music competition between the Sirens and the Muses. The Muses won and, failing to show any magnanimity, pulled off the Siren's wings who then drowned and became the islands in the bay.

The city walls are still visible in parts and were once 4km ($2^1/_2$ miles) long. The flat area in the middle of the site is the centre of the city where remains of a second-century temple have been found. An 'L'-shaped building used to house Roman cisterns and there are traces of a theatre. The site was destroyed by Arab raiders but reoccupied in the Byzantine period.

The main road leads straight into Hania with a turning towards Souda and the Akrotiri Peninsula. The Souda route passes through the military base where there are not only restrictions on photography, but also on parking or stopping within the base.

# • Places of Interest Between Rethimnon and the Akrotiri Peninsula

**Gerani**
A cave in the hillside above the only reasonable beach in the immediate area.

**Asigonia**
A mountain village famous for its folk songs.

**Lake Kournas**
The only natural lake on the island. Its clear waters lie below high mountains.

**Georgioupolis**
A resort at the end of a long, sandy beach.

**Aptera**
An ancient Greek site covering a wide area with a Turkish fort in the vicinity and good views over the bay.

**Souda War Cemetery**
The Allied cemetery looking out over the bay with over 1,500 immaculate graves.

**Venizelos Graves**
The burial place of Venizelos and his son, overlooking Hania.

**Stavros**
The best beach on the Akrotiri Peninsula, at the far tip.

**Ayia Triadha**
A seventeenth-century monastery.

**Gouverneto/Katholiko**
Two monasteries, the monks moved from the latter to the former to avoid pirates.

**Souda** itself is just beyond here and is a typical port area. This is where the ferries from Piraeus dock and the most sensible course after disembarkation seems to be to head straight into Hania. There are frequent buses to the city from Souda.

Just out of Souda, heading into the peninsula, is a turning off right to the Allied War Cemetery. It is an impressive and deeply moving  place, with its lush green grass, in total contrast to the dusty scrubland all around it, and the blue of the Mediterranean beyond. It seems very much a corner of England in a foreign field. There is a large cross at the centre and the graves are in rows on either side, each surrounded by flowers.

A small porch at the entrance gives an account of the battles and the numbers killed and has a register of all those who are buried here. There are 1,527 graves and about half of them are British; of the

*A bay on the south side of Akrotiri Peninsula*

remainder, 447 are New Zealanders and 197 Australians.

✳ Across the peninsula are the **Venizelos Graves**; a specially created memorial park where Eleftherios Venizelos and his son are
buried. Their graves lie on the site where the Greek flag was first
raised on Crete in 1897 in defiance of the Turks, becoming yet another
symbolic site for the independence movement. Venizelos was the
much-revered Cretan statesman who fought for Independence and
later *Enosis* (union with Greece). He was Prime Minister of Greece
several times, although he was ultimately forced to resign and flee
into exile when his Republican views offended the monarchist mood
on the mainland. He died in France in 1936. The setting of the
memorial is magnificent, with views back across Hania, and the
simple stone slabs which mark the graves make a moving monument. Also in the grounds is the little chapel of Prophitis Ilias.

The best beaches on the Akrotiri Peninsula are on its western side.
They are accessible from the road which runs a short distance inland.
**Kalathas** is an attractive place and clearly a growing resort with a
pleasant beach. As with all places on the peninsula, visitors will have
to put up with the noise of the fighters from the base which practise
in the area.

✳ Right at the tip of the peninsula is **Stavros Beach**. It lies in a small
bay, dominated on one side by the bulk of a mountain in which there
is a cave visible from the beach. Excavation revealed the remains of
a religious sanctuary. There are a few tavernas but little else and it
should be a quiet place unless there is a coach trip from one of the
resorts.

There is little access to the other side of the peninsula because of
the military base, although there is one beach at the far seaward end
by the site of *Minoa*. This is not, as one might think, a Minoan
settlement but the Classical port for *Aptera*. On the way down to the
beach there are views of the Island of Souda on which there are
Venetian and Turkish fortifications. Indeed, this island stronghold
held out against the Turks for many years after the huge city forts had
fallen.

The peninsula also contains two important monasteries, the first
being that of Ayia Triadha (Aghia Triada) which is on a dusty track
beyond the airport. It dates from the early seventeenth century and
was built by a Venetian called Zangarola. It has a domed church at
its centre but its once-elaborate buildings have fallen into disrepair.

Beyond here is the Gouverneto Monastery, 4km (2¹/₂ miles)

away on a track which, although tarmac in parts, remains quite rough. The monks probably moved inland to this building from the Katholiko Monastery, which lies on the coast, to avoid the attention of pirates. The Katholiko ruins are accessible only on foot, about 45 minutes' walk from Gouverneto.

After about 15 minutes, the Arkouditissa Cave of Artemis is reached. Religious relics were found here relating to the worship of this goddess. From here the path becomes quite steep and it is still some way to the monastery which was built in the cliff face and abandoned 300 years ago under the onslaught of the pirates.

Near the monastery is another cave, which is the grave of St John the Hermit, a very early Evangelist who came to the island when it was recaptured by the Byzantine Empire from the Arabs. The cave is very dark and slippery. It is possible to walk on from here to the sea and swim from the rocks.

# 9
# *HANIA*

Hania (Chania, Khania) lies towards the western end of the island about 1 hour's drive from Rethimnon on the new road. It has its own airport on the Akrotiri Peninsula and a ferry port in Souda Bay, one of the best deepwater anchorages in the Mediterranean. The city makes a viable alternative to Iraklion as a point of arrival in the country, as well as a suitable base for exploring the mountainous west of the island.

Modern Hania is believed to be on the site of ancient *Kydonia*. According to legend, the city was founded by Kydon, King Minos' grandson. The Kastelli area of the city has been extensively excavated and produced finds of Neolithic pottery, signs of Bronze Age settlement and Minoan tombs. These were unusual for being found so far west, as most Minoan settlement seems to have been concentrated in the east of the island. While nothing as spectacular as the other Minoan palaces has been found, *Kydonia* does seem to have been a significant Minoan site.

It is possible that the Myceneans based their occupation here after the destruction of *Knossos* and Homer mentions that Menelaus' fleet, returning from Troy, was shipwrecked at *Kydonia*. This is only one of several references to the city in Classical literature. Clearly, *Kydonia* was an important city state in the post Minoan period, minting its own coins and dominating the western region of the island.

After leading the resistance against the Romans, it was captured and became one of their leading cities on the island. It retained this role during the Byzantine period but from this point Hania seems to have entered a troubled period in its history with repeated pirate raids causing much destruction.

*The attractive narrow streets of Hania*

Even Venetian rule did not bring peace. The Genoese, great enemies of the Venetians and rivals for the control of Crete, captured the city and ruled over it for more than 20 years. The situation was further complicated when the Venetian rulers had to deal not only with native insurrection, but also that of their own settlers who rebelled in 1268 and 1363.

Prosperity finally came with the Venetian reassertion of power and much new building took place including that of the fortifications. These were designed by Sammichele, the engineer who built Iraklion's walls, with the same purpose of deterring pirate raids by Barbarossa. However, these defensive installations proved to be of little use against the Turkish attack in 1645 when the city surrendered very quickly.

While Turkish occupation was much resented, the combination of the numerical superiority which the Muslim population soon established and severe reprisals for any resistance meant that Hania remained relatively peaceful during this period. This was typical of the whole island; the Turks managed to subdue the towns but resistance continued to threaten them from the mountains.

In 1898, with the end of Turkish rule and the handover to the Great Powers (France, Britain, Italy and Russia), Hania became the island's capital, a title which it retained until 1971 when Iraklion took over this role.

Independence had been gained partly as a result of the exchange of fire involving British soldiers, caused by the raising of the Greek flag on a hill above Hania. The city remained very much in the forefront of the continuing conflict as the struggle for union with Greece intensified.

Venizelos, the Cretan politician who is much associated with Hania, set up a revolutionary assembly in nearby Theriso to oppose rule by the Great powers and there were riots in the city. As a result, Prince George resigned as High Commissioner and a few years later, in 1913, the island became part of Greece. The Greek flag was now legitimately raised in Hania's Firka Tower.

Then, in 1941, came the German airborne assault which enjoyed its greatest success at Maleme, just west of Hania. The city suffered severe bombardment, not least because of its proximity to Souda Bay which then, as now, was of strategic importance both to the defenders and the attackers.

Hania has been rebuilt and has sprawling modern suburbs which

# Places of Interest in Hania

**Harbour**
The Venetian harbour is in two parts, the outer harbour is now devoted to tourist cafés, the inner still works as a port with a Venetian lighthouse at the end of the harbour wall.

**Firkas**
The home of the Naval Museum and the best place to start exploring the city walls which once stretched around the whole city.

**Zambeliou**
The road running parallel to the harbour. Full of old houses and pleasant narrow alleys leading into the heart of the old town.

**Mosque of the Janissaries**
Built by the Turks, this odd-looking, domed building is now the tourist office.

**Kastelli**
The oldest part of the city where excavations have revealed Minoan tombs.

**Archaeological Museum**
Housed in the old San Fransisco church, it contains exhibits of local finds from Neolithic to Roman times.

**Halidon/Skridlof**
The main shopping areas in Hania, the latter being full of shops selling leather goods.

**Indoor Market**
An abundance of produce in this cruciform covered market with a very lively and noisy atmosphere.

**Plateia 1821**
A bishop was hanged here in 1821. The churches of Ayios Nikolaos with its headless minaret, San Rocco and Ayia Anargyri can be found nearby.

**Historical Museum**
Reached after a long walk heading out of town past the Public Gardens, it has documents covering all periods of the city's history.

**Beach**
The beach is to the west of the city and has all the usual facilities.

house its population of 50,000, along with a rumoured population of 750,000 sheep and goats. This makes navigating through or around the city particularly difficult.

Parking also poses problems, especially near the harbour, and the best places to find unrestricted parking are in the streets away from the sea, beyond the market.

Accommodation is easy to find in Hania; there is a profusion of

*Sunset over the harbour, Hania*

rent rooms and several hotels near the harbour. The former only seem to be crowded at the very height of the season or during late May at the time of the Festival of the Battle of Crete.

There are large numbers of restaurants on the quays of the outer harbour and these are the most obvious attraction for tourists. However, the inner harbour should not be ignored and, in the side streets beyond the Arsenali, there are other places to eat which tend to be cheaper and have more local colour.

The city is known for its fish and a walk along the harbour may offer the sight of fish being unloaded or squid draped over a broom handle drying in the evening sun before ending up in the restaurant behind.

The main bus station is on Kidonias, on the far side of the Plateia 1866 at the top of Halidon and not far from the major sites of interest.

The ferry port is at Souda with regular bus connections to the centre of town. There are daily ferries to Athens and less frequent services to other islands.

The airport is on the Akrotiri Peninsula 13km (8 miles) east of the city and reasonably well-signposted. The runway is shared with the fighters of the military base which dominates the west of the peninsula. As at Iraklion, there are few facilities other than a small café and duty-free shop but it is very much a secondary airport for holiday flights and much of the chaos caused by the crowds at Iraklion is avoided here.

✳ The **Old City** within the walls is the most attractive part of Hania and is divided into five areas. Kastelli is on the hill above the harbour where the Minoan remains have been found. Hiones lies at the eastern end of the harbour. Splanzia covers the south and heart of the city. Evraiki is the region round the outer harbour where most of the facilities for tourists are found. Topanas is the area behind the harbour containing some of the best-preserved Venetian houses. Finally, the Khalepa district lies in a suburb to the east of the city which was made fashionable by Prince George during his brief period as ruler at the beginning of this century.

✳ The harbour is the focus of any visit to Hania. Hotels and restaurants are ranged around its quays and horses in straw hats pull weary tourists around in brightly painted carriages. The heart of the outer harbour is the Syntrivani Square. This is now surrounded by cafés and there is a concealed Venetian fountain behind the outside stairs of the Plaza Hotel.

At the seaward end of the harbour is the **Firkas**, the name of both the tower and this part of the defensive walls. These are best-preserved on this western side of the city; the Turkish bombardment having taken in its toll on the other walls. As a result, they do not dominate the city in the same way as they do in Iraklion. The walls took 12 years to build and are over 3km (2miles) long with a moat 10m (32ft) deep on the landward side and four bastions. The most visible survivor is the Shiavo Bastion in the heart of the old city, reached on any number of dusty paths which cross the area.

In the bastion of the Firkas is the **Naval Museum** of Crete, opened in 1973 and which contains reproductions of ships, weapons and a large collection of sea shells. In the courtyard, in front of the museum, there are occasional performances of Greek drama. The Firkas is a symbolic site because it was here, in 1913, that the Greek flag was first raised legitimately on the island after union with Greece.

Behind this western quayside are some of the most attractive and atmospheric areas of the city. **Zambeliou** is a narrow street with several Venetian houses still standing. The road leads to progressively narrower alleys, through the Renieri Gate, a decorated Venetian archway, to little exclusive craft shops, quieter restaurants and flower bedecked gardens. It is an extremely pleasant place to stroll and discover unexpected bits of city wall, dusty paths and picturesque doorways; all of which contribute to the unique atmosphere.

Returning to the harbour, the most striking sight is the **Mosque of Janissaries,** with its odd-looking dome and arches. It was built by the Turks in 1645 when they captured the city and was extensively damaged during World War II but is now restored and serves as the tourist office.

Around the corner behind the inner harbour is the Kastelli area of the city where most of the archaeological excavation has taken place. It is here that Neolithic remains were found with a Minoan settlement on top. The most important site is on **Kanevaro** where a number of Minoan tombs were discovered. On **Odhos Lithinon,** a Minoan house is being uncovered and all around the area are reminders of the Venetian period. At No 45 is the site of the former Venetian archive which bears an inscription dating from 1623.

The inner harbour is still used by visiting yachts and fishing boats and has all the paraphernalia of a working port, including a customs house and a ship's chandlers. The arches of the Venetian Arsenali (drydocks) are still visible and reaonably well-preserved.

*Hania in the evening sunshine*

    An interesting walk, although one which is longer than it first appears, is out along the harbour wall to the lighthouse. This was another Venetian edifice, restored by the Egyptians during their brief period here at the beginning of the last century. The path can be uneven and does lead through the middle of a restaurant but there is a way through and the views back across the harbour and out to sea make it worthwhile.

**Halidon** is one of the main shopping streets in Hania with all the usual range of tourist souvenir shops. A short distance away from  the harbour on the right is the **Archaeological Museum** in the old Venetian church of San Fransisco. It is no longer very impressive

from the front but the interior and the gardens alongside are pleasant and much restored. The building dates from the sixteenth century; the Turks converted it to a mosque on their arrival and the base of the minaret is visible in the garden, along with a fountain of the same period.

The exhibits are of local finds and follow a chronological order starting with Neolithic artefacts; a substantial amount of Minoan pottery, including several giant pithoi (large storage urns), and the tablets found in Kastelli which bear examples of both Linear A and Linear B script. In the centre of the room are Minoan tombs (*Larnakes*) complete with skeletons from the Armeni cemetery near Rethimnon. There are also a number of Graeco-Roman sculptures, mosaics and pottery.

Opposite the museum, in a dusty square with a yellow temporary post office cabin, is the **Triymartyri Cathedral** which was built towards the end of the last century. Also visible in the corner of the square are the domes of a building which was once a Turkish bath.

The second left beyond the cathedral is Skridlof, where the leather shops are concentrated. Hania is a good place for buying presents; leather shoes and bags of all shapes and sizes are available in virtually every shop in the street. The manufacture of the goods still goes on in the back of these shops in between the energetic salesmanship. Hania is also known for its distinctive blue clay pottery which is on sale in the many craft shops around the city. These shops have much more attractive souvenirs than those usually offered in tourist shops, although the inevitable T shirts and table mats are still widely available.

As the road moves into Tsouderon, the indoor market comes into view. It is a huge building in the shape of a cross and sells every imaginable produce from meat to dairy produce or fruit.

Beyond the market, on the left, is a minaret without a mosque and heading back towards the harbour are the narrow streets which make up the Splanzia district. **Ayios Nikolaos Church** is in the Plateia 1821, it was built by the Venetians, as part of a monastery and later converted to a mosque. It has both a bell tower and a minaret, the latter being easily recognisable because it lacks a top. The building was only converted back to an Orthodox church in 1912.

The square is named to commemorate the hanging of a bishop here by the Turks during a revolt against them. At the far end of the square, which is now lined with cafés, is the little Venetian church of San Rocco dating from 1630 but now closed. Nearby is Ayia Anargia, a small Orthodox church built in the sixteenth century and which functioned even during the Turkish occupation.

At the other side of the Old City are the Public Gardens which contain a small zoo. They are some distance from the old town, as is the **Historical Museum** which is beyond the park.

The museum has two floors of exhibits, one room is devoted to Eleftherios Venizelos, the Cretan politician who was active in the Independence movement and later became Prime Minister of Greece. He is buried in a specially created park which overlooks Hania. Upstairs are examples of Venetian furniture and documents covering most periods of the city's history but focusing on the resistance to the Turks and later the Germans. It also has a folklore collection with examples of weaving and other local crafts.

The Khalepa district is a fairly modern area at the eastern end of the town. It became fashionable when Prince George set up residence here and the area contains a large number of grand old houses. Some way from the harbour is Dhikastrion Square which has the obligatory statue of Venizelos and the Law Courts which were once the headquarters of the Great Powers administration. Those seeking to complete the various Venizelos pilgrimages could continue on Venizelos Street away from the city, passing the house where Prince George lived. Opposite this residence is Venizelos' house, not open to the public and still owned by the family. There is another statue in the little square on the other side of the road.

From here it is a short drive to the Akrotiri Peninsula and the Venizelos Graves which are marked by stone slabs in a park overlooking the town. (This area is described in more detail in the previous chapter.)

The town beach is about 10 minutes on foot from the Firkas heading westward, passing the swimming pool. It is often quite crowded but it is long enough for everyone to find a space if they walk far enough. It has several cafés, some watersports and a small islet offshore adds interest to the landscape.

Holiday development continues along this coast and several beaches are accessible, Ayia Apostoli being the most widely publicised place. Beyond here the development runs in a continous strip to Platanias. (For more detail on this see the next chapter).

The number of specific places of interest to visit in Hania is limited. However, it is a pleasant city to wander around and either despair at the ruinous and shabby state of much of its historic buildings or revel in its natural atmosphere as a city that has a life of its own outside the tourist season.

*Church in Hania*

# 10
# *WESTERN CRETE*

This region of the island is dominated by the Levka Ori Mountains, also known as the White Mountains because of their distinctive colour. The mountains, which descend steeply to the southern shore, mean that a substantial part of this coast is accessible only on foot or by boat. This is the area known as Sfakia, notorious for the ferocity of its people in their opposition to the various enemies that have occupied the island, as well as for some lawlessness among themselves. It is claimed that there are more policemen per head of population in Sfakia than anywhere else in Crete.

The area sees less tourists than the eastern end of the island; the landscape can seem more forbidding and the villages run down, lacking the prosperity brought by the tourists. Although this looks set to change, any mass tourist development will be severely limited by the simple geography of the place which offers a very different and distinctive experience of Crete.

## Hania to Kolimvari

The coastal road west out of Hania can scarcely claim to be unspoiled, with continuous strip development on both sides of the road. The beach is never far away but can be difficult to reach through the closely packed construction.

It is not until **Ayia Marina** that there is a village that can be seen as a specific entity, independent of Hania. It has a campsite at the western end of its beach from where the island of Ayii Theodori is visible. The island is now a nature reserve for the rare Cretan mountain goat, the agrimi or kri-kri. According to legend, the island represents a whale that tried to swallow Crete and was turned to stone for its pains.

**Platanias**, 11km (7 miles) from Hania, is a more sizeable place; the old village is perched precariously on the hillside, while the tourist development stretches along the main road. A small car park in the centre of the village houses the temporary post office cabin and the phone office.

There are plenty of restaurants, some of which are the focus of tours from Hania, and several good souvenir shops selling pottery and leather goods. There are also rooms to rent concentrated at the eastern end of the village. The beach is accessible from the main road along any of the dirt tracks between the houses. Beyond Platanias it becomes more difficult to get to the sea as there are fields between the shore and the road with few tracks to join them.

**Maleme** is the next village west and is where the German parachutists had early success in the Battle of Crete when they captured the airfield and the infamous Hill 107. This was the only place where the airborne assault had any success and the German Commander wrote later, 'I decided to concentrate all our forces against one spot. We selected Maleme because at least here we could see a glimmer of light.' It was the resulting failure of the counter attack here that led to the controversial Allied decision to evacuate the island.

❋ The German War Cemetery is on the hill behind the village, some distance down a narrow road. The turning marked 'Deutsche Friedhof' is opposite a large hotel and easy to miss. The road then climbs the hill, passing the site of a Minoan tomb.

There is a café at the entrance to the cemetery and a few places to park. Inside is a porch with an outline of the main events of the battle on the wall along with details as to the number of dead. There are 4,465 men buried here. The graves are a short way up the hill; the gravestones lying flat among the incredibly lush grass and the red of the mesembryanthemum flowers. A tall cross stands at the end of the cemetery looking out over the airfield to the shore, creating a particularly poignant perspective. Whether by accident or design, none of this is visible from the road.

The airfield is now a military base past which the main road runs out to Tavronitis where the road across the island to Paleohora begins. (This route is described later). **Tavronitis** itself is a small farming village with a few holiday developments and a pebbly

## Places of Interest
## Between Hania and Kolimvari

**Platanias**
A holiday resort with a good beach and souvenir shops and an interesting old section on the hill behind.

**Maleme**
War Cemetery
The German war cemetery with 4,500 carefully tended graves on a hill where some of the fiercest fighting took place.

**Kolimvari**
A quiet village at the end of a superb beach with a picturesque little harbour.

**Moni Gonia**
Impressive seventeenth-century monastery in a fine setting with a Turkish cannonball lodged in its walls.

**Diktynnaion**
Accessible only by boat, the site of a Greek temple to the huntress goddess Dyktinna.

beach. Beyond Tavronitis are several large hotels by the beach and some distinctive blue-domed churches peculiar to this part of the island.

**Kolimvari** is a short distance off the main road towards the sea. It has a small harbour and lies at the western end of a long beach which, although pebbly, is clean and pleasant. There are a few rooms available and even a building which claims to be a hotel but the village remains very quiet with a tranquil atmosphere.

Just outside Kolimvari, heading up the Rodopou Peninsula, is the Moni Gonia, a monastery with a picturesque exterior looking out over the bay. It is closed from 12.30 to 4.30pm for siesta and the usual dress rules apply. The monastery was visited in the 1830s by Robert Pashley, the English writer, who recorded in his book, *Travels in Crete*, that he was much impressed by the quality of the wine offered to him but distinctly unimpressed by the intelligence of the monks who served it.

The current building of the monastery dates from the early seventeenth century and contains several important icons from this period as well as some later examples. In one corner of the courtyard is a small museum with displays of historical documents and the

*The Levka Ori Mountains*

more valuable icons. Despite the cannonball lodged in the seaward wall, the monastery escaped relatively unscathed from the Turkish invasion.

The view from these seaward walls is particularly impressive and the monastery's setting is central to its attraction. On the other side of the road is an eighteenth-century fountain behind which, up the hill, are the remains of the original thirteenth-century church of the monastery.

The road then continues further into the peninsula with good coastal views until it turns inland to the village of Afrata where the asphalt section stops. The peninsula can be further explored on the road to Rodopou village but beyond here any further excursions have to be made on foot or by boat. Boats can be hired from Kolimvari to go to *Dyktinnaion* (*Diktynaion*) on the far tip of the peninsula. This is the site of a temple to the huntress goddess, Dyktinna, who seems to have been another manifestation of Artemis. It was excavated during the war by German archaeologists and revealed a structure with Ionic and Corinthian columns.

The only other place of interest on the peninsula is the church of

Ayios Ioannis (Aghios Joanis), visited annually by pilgrims on the Saint's day on 29 August. The bad track is not really viable for cars so a good $2^1/_2$ hour walk is necessary to reach the church.

## The Far West

The road from Kolimvari to Kastelli can be surprisingly busy and the large numbers of lorries on its narrow bends make it a dangerous drive. Initially it stays close to the coast, passing through various seaside villages. Of these, **Drapanias** is the biggest and has the most tourist development, including a campsite near the beach.

From here the road climbs into the hills in series of sharp bends and at the top the coast to Kastelli becomes visible. At Kaloudiana there is a turning inland for an exploration of the hills and the far south-west, an area which is described later.

**Kastelli Kisamou** has undergone various changes of name to avoid confusion with other Kastellis. It is sometimes known by both or either of the above, with signposts lacking any consistency on the matter. It was the site of fierce fighting in the Battle of Crete and when the town fell amid rumours of mutilation of German soldiers, the Germans took a terrible revenge by killing 200 local men.

The town itself is a straggly, rather grey place with the main road running through it. It has a pebbly beach, numerous hotels and restaurants but little to recommend it for a long stay.

It was a port for the Classical city of *Polyrinia* and was prosperous during Roman times, even Ptolemy seemed to have heard of it, but today there are no remains of the town's history.

*Polyrinia* itself, which is 7km (4 miles) inland from Kastelli, is impressively situated in the mountains on a path beyond the village of Ano Paleokastro. The ancient city has all but disappeared but there are plenty of relics from later periods including an aqueduct, which is probably Roman, and Venetian fortifications.

The Gramvousa Peninsula, the far spike of the island, has no roads or tracks and the only habitation past or present was on the offshore island of Imeri Gramvousa where the Venetians built a fortress.

The main road therefore, runs west out of Kastelli but soon turns south to the village of Platanos where there are several signs to *Falasarna* (on the right if coming from Kastelli). The official sign is 100m (330ft) beyond the hand-painted one but both head in the right direction.

The descent to the coast offers stunning views of the turquoise sea and white sand below, the beauty of which is somewhat marred by the number of plastic greenhouses in the area.

At the junction, turn right along the coast where there are a couple of beaches accessible down tracks; look for the parked cars to determine their exact location. The main beach is the cove where the road stops at the northern end of the bay where there are a few tavernas and some rooms to rent.

This is the site of the ancient city state of *Falasarna* (*Phalasarna*), the traditional enemy of *Polyrinia*. Any ruins, however, are very difficult to find and spread over a large area. Most easily identifiable are the stone throne, just beyond the tavernas, and the harbour, now a flattened area. This is now well-inland and proves that the western end of the island has tilted up over 8m (26ft) since the harbour was in use.

The beach is the main attraction of *Falasarna* with its beautifully

## Places of Interest in The Far West

**Kastelli**
A town with a pebbly beach and a few hotels by the sea.

*Polyrinia*
Impressively situated in the mountains on a path beyond Ano Paleokastro. The site of an ancient city state, also inhabited by the Romans and the Venetians.

**Falasarna**
A beautiful beach with clear water and sparkling sand.

**Sfinari**
A small, coastal village in one of the most isolated parts of the island.

**Hrisoskalitissa**
A monastery with ninety steps, one of which is supposedly made of gold but only visible to those without sin.

**Elafonisi**
Isolated, idyllic beach with shallow, clear waters and offshore islands.

clear water, which must be the coldest in Crete, and fine white sand. The only drawbacks which might spoil this idyllic setting are that tar can occasionally be washed up on the shore and the fact that its charms are not a well-kept secret and the beach can become crowded.

South of Platanos, the road continues for 18km (11miles) to Sfinari through a wild, uninhabited stretch of countryside with incredible views down the sheer cliffs. **Sfinari** itself is a village close  to the sea with a whole maze of rough tracks leading eventually to the beach.

From here it is possible to continue southwards and ultimately arrive at Kefali and then complete a circuit by driving back to the Kastelli road. This is an interesting excursion but has the major drawback that much of this route to Kefali is unpaved. However, the perils of this may be outweighed by the spectacular views on this  section of road and the sheer isolation of the region. Even the villages seem half abandoned, save for the old crones who have been known to flag down tourist cars, not to warn of landslips ahead but to plead for spare drachmas.

The tarred road stops at **Kambos** and is unpaved in between the villages and tarmac within them, the reverse of the usual Cretan pattern. This means there is a 4km (2$^1/_2$miles) stretch unpaved, 1km ($^3/_4$ mile) tarmac, 2km (1$^1/_2$ miles) unpaved, a short tarmac section

*The German War Cemetery near Maleme*

*The harbour at Kolimvari*

*The church of Ayios Ioannis*

and then 5km (3 miles) unpaved before the track becomes a reasonable road at Kefali. Here there is refreshment available for the exhausted driver.

The alternative route up to this village is to turn off the Kastelli road at Kaloudiana and climb up to Topolia and, just beyond it, the cave of Ayia Sophia. This lies high in the cliff above the road and is reached up a series of steps. There is a small chapel in the cave along with various stalactites and stalagmites.

The route now passes through a spectacular ravine and there is the rare opportunity on Crete to pass through a tunnel which is unlit so hire car drivers need to locate the switch for their headlights.

Beyond the gorge is a more fertile valley known for its chestnut trees. **Elos**, a quiet village, is the local centre for this crop and holds a festival when they are harvested.

At Kefali is the turning south to the Hrisoskalitissa Monastery which is 10km (6 miles) away on a dirt road. The nunnery is not particularly old although there has been a church here since the thirteenth century. The original church was built inside a grotto. The path up to the church is marked by ninety steps, one of which is supposed to appear gold to those without sin.

5km (3 miles) beyond the convent, on a deteriorating track, is **Elafonisi**. This is a veritable paradise beach with an island offshore sheltering the beach and adding to its tropical lagoon-like qualities with clear sea and white sand. Its isolation is under threat from the boat trips bringing visitors here for the day. Admittedly, this does make it possible for many more people to enjoy the place and is an attractive alternative to the difficult drive.

## Inland from Hania

The area just inland from Hania offers the opportunity for several rewarding short excursions, the best of which is to **Theriso** which is reputedly the birthplace of Venizelos' mother. Venizelos was a much revered Cretan politician who was active in the Independence movement. However, it is not the village which is the main interest here but the drive itself, through the Theriso Gorge. It is a very narrow, pretty ravine with several caves in the cliffs and places to have a picnic. The village is small and of little interest but the starting point for a pleasant walk across to another pretty mountain village; Meskla.

Another Venizelos monument in the area is at **Mournies**, where he lived for some time. However, apart from the plaque on the wall, there is little to see. On a dirt track near Mournies is the fine old Hrisopigi Monastery with fortified walls and a spring at the centre of its courtyard.

The other road in the region known for its mountain scenery is that which leads up to **Omalos**, seen by most people from a bus on their way to the Samaria Gorge. The road is difficult to find from Hania; although there are sporadic signs to the gorge, care should be taken to avoid turning inland too soon.

The correct road climbs to **Alikianou**, 12km (7$^1$/$_2$ miles) from Hania, where the left fork should be taken to Omalos. At Fourne, a detour can be taken to Meskla which passes one of the many war memorials in the region. **Meskla** is known for a much earlier rebellion against the Venetians. This was the Kandaleneon Revolt, around which a whole series of myths has grown up. Apparently, with the whole of the west of the island taking part in the insurrection, the rebels set up an administrative base here and were only captured when the Venetian army surprised them after a riotous night of feasting held to celebrate the marriage of Kandaleneon's son.

Back on the main road is **Lakki** (Laki), a picturesque mountain village with a memorial to the New Zealander, D.C. Perkins, who became a folk hero among the locals for his exploits in organising resistance to the Germans. He was killed leading an ambush in 1944 and was buried in Lakki.

The **Omalos Plateau**, 44km (27 miles) from Hania, is an odd bowl-shaped region quite unlike any other plateau on the island. It is also much higher, being at a height of 1,050m (3,444ft). The plain is covered with snow in winter and turns into marshy ground in spring but in summer shepherds bring their flocks up here and a potato crop is produced. Some of the most spectacular mountains in Crete are visible from the plateau, Pahnes, at 2,452m (8,042ft), being the highest, and the region is a prime centre for those wishing to climb some of these peaks. Alternatively, a less strenuous option is walking on the plateau itself, it takes about 1 hour to walk from one end to the other.

Most people, however, come here not to climb but to descend; just beyond the village of Omalos, is Xiloskalo; the head of the Samaria Gorge.

# Samaria Gorge

## PRACTICAL INFORMATION

In every resort on the island trips are advertised to the **Samaria Gorge**; trips which manage to stir holidaymakers from the sun, sand and sea, so much so that they are prepared to attempt a 6 hour hike on a blazing hot day which usually necessitates getting up at 5.30am to make the trip.

Admittedly, all 16km (10miles) are downhill but this does not mean that the walk does not require a certain fitness or that it is completely without danger. In October 1988, two British tourists were killed and many stranded when storms caused a huge torrent of water to flood the gorge with catastrophic results. The gorge is closed to the public from November to April but at the beginning and end of the season the trip should not be attempted if there is any threat of rain.

The organised tours have their own buses at either end and are usually accompanied by 'guides' whose local knowledge or even common sense should not be relied upon.

For those visitors wishing to travel independently and avoid some of the crowds, even though solitude is impossible in summer, there is a scheduled bus service from Hania bus station to the start of the gorge. These buses leave at 06.00, 08.30, 09.30 and 16.30; the early bus having the obvious advantage that walkers can benefit from the coolest part of the day. The bus journey to the starting point takes about $1^1/_2$ hours.

The national park which covers the gorge is open from 6am to 3pm, after that visitors are only allowed in the first 2km (1 mile) at either end. There are wardens in the park who are supposed to check this and who hand out tickets with the date on at the start which is handed in at the bottom to check that nobody is left in overnight. Camping in the gorge is not allowed. In practice, the ticket system is only erratically enforced.

There are numerous other rules, mainly connected with preventing fires and preserving the wildlife and the plants. The park is a refuge for the rare kri-kri mountain goat but they are unlikely to stray near the path.

In summer very little should be carried and light clothing is all that is needed but it may be quite cold at the top in the early morning. Decent, comfortable footwear is absolutely essential. Although

*Walking in the Samaria Gorge*

about a thousand people walk down the gorge daily in training shoes (probably the best option) and without mishap, it is really a case of being sensible; it is not the place to twist an ankle. What is certain is that it pays to stop to admire the view. Early or late in the season a pullover and waterproof seem advisable.

Drinking water is available from springs, especially in the early part of the gorge but in summer a water bottle could prove useful.

The walk ends at the village of Ayia Roumeli from where there is a regular boat service to Hora Sfakion which connects up with the buses to Hania. The boat times are 09.15, 14.30, 15.45, 17.00 and 18.00; note that the 17.00 boat is the last one which has a guaranteed connection with the bus and that not all these boats run in low season. Times should therefore be checked before setting out, bearing in mind it will take 5 to 6 hours to do the walk.

The boat back takes about 1 hour, more if it stops at Loutro, and the buses back to Hania should leave at 07.00, 11.00, 16.00 and 18.30; they will wait for the boat if it is late.

Alternative ways of exploring the gorge are to climb up it or to take one of the tours advertised as 'Samaria The Easy Way'; these bring people by boat to Ayia Roumeli from where they walk through the lower part of the gorge as far as the Iron Gates, its narrowest point.

### THE WALK ITSELF

The gorge starts at Xiloskalo where there is a tourist pavilion which serves food and, occasionally, one of its seven beds are available. There are also stalls selling food and drink which tends to be expensive.

The start of the gorge is down a purpose-built wooden staircase, after which Xiloskalo is named, and which descends rapidly through pine trees to the river bed. The gorge is wide here and only becomes a true ravine later. Nonetheless, its walls are truly spectacular. If you have not taken plenty of film you will be regretting it within a few minutes.

The path begins to follow the course of the River Tarraios, crossing it from time to time depending on the season, as the volume of water in the gorge is obviously markedly different in August to that in May. After 5km (3 miles), a tributary joins the river and the gorge changes direction, now heading south towards the sea.

The path continues to follow the river before climbing up above the right bank. Some 15 minutes walk from the change in direction, at about 7km (4miles), is the village of **Samaria**, across a bridge on the opposite bank of the river. There is a warden's house here and some toilets. The village is very old, dating from the fourteenth century, but was abandoned in 1962 to facilitate the creation of the park. Nearby is the church of Osia Maria which is thought to be the origin of the name of the gorge. The church was built in 1379 and still contains early frescoes.

Beyond Samaria, the gorge narrows slightly and the path joins the river at intervals, making it necessary to use the boulders in the river bed as stepping stones. This is not always easy if there is a lot of water flowing through. The path then regains the higher ground as the gorge narrows and widens periodically.

The Iron Gates or *Sidheresportes* are the highlight of the walk. They form the narrowest part of the gorge, the dimensions of which were graphically described by Robert Pashley, the English traveller who passed through here on a mule in the early nineteenth century. He declared 'The width of this lofty chasm is about ten feet at the ground and widens to about thirty or at the most forty feet at the top. The length of the way along which we have to pass in the middle of the rapid stream is about sixty paces.' The simple measurements can only hint at the dramatic perspective the sheer, smoothed rock presents in this most spectacular part of the gorge.

The valley now widens out, leading down to another abandoned village, that of **Ayia Roumeli** which has been relocated to the shore. A little further on is a wooden gate which has a sign saying 'You have now reached the end of the gorge' in a dozen different languages, each ostensibly signed by the respective leaders of the relevant country. This is not quite the end as it is about another 1km ($^1/_2$ mile) to the village, where most of the walker's needs are catered for. Cold drinks, a pleasant beach and rooms offering the ultimate luxury of 'hot water' constitute the total of Ayia Roumeli's attractions.

The boat ride to Hora Sfakion should be a relaxing finale to the trip with dramatic views of the mountains from which the walker has just emerged.

Hora Sfakion is a small village which caters for the trade generated by the gorge. There are numerous restaurants, souvenir shops and rooms to rent. In the evening, when this trade has moved on, the village is very quiet. (For a more detailed description see the South of Rethimnon chapter).

*The entrance to the Samaria Gorge*

## Routes to the South Coast

There are two main roads which cross the island in this region, one which goes to Souyia (Sougia), 70km (43miles) from Hania, the other going to Paleohora, 57km (35miles) from Tavronitis.

The road to Souyia is very badly signposted; follow signs to the gorge and Omalos and take the furthest west of the roads going inland from Hania. The road forks at **Alikianou**, a village just off the road which has an old fourteenth-century church. For Souyia, take the right-hand fork.

The countryside is particularly lush in this area and quite unlike the vegetation normally found in the Mediterranean. However, the road then begins to climb into the mountains and this new perspective offers a startling contrast with what has gone before. These mountains are particularly barren and display strange rock formations.

There are very few villages to break up the landscape which is so desolate it can only support a few goats. The road climbs and descends frequently, making for a long and tiring drive.

Rodovani lies at the top of the final pass and marks the way across

*The Iron Gates, Samaria Gorge*

to Paleohora, although the major highway marked on some maps is not yet completed. The village of Maralia marks the site of ancient *Elyros* (*Elypos*). Despite being one of the most important Classical sites in the region, nothing has yet been excavated. The main road now descends the final 10km (6 miles) to the coast and **Souyia**. It is something of a surprise to discover that such a major road, which clearly required much effort to build, should lead to such a tiny place. There are a few rooms to rent, as well as the odd restaurant and a single shop, but very little else.

The only site of any interest is the Byzantine church and the remains of its mosaic but most of this has been obliterated by the modern one built on top of it and the mosaic has been removed to Hania for conservation. The modern church was built on divine instructions, revealed by a villager who slept on the site and received a vision urging him to construct the new building. As the latter church is usually locked, there is very little to see. The port for the ancient Greek city of *Elyros* (*Elypos*) was here but nothing remains of this today.

In archaeological terms, a more interesting place is *Lissos*, accessible only on foot and about 1 hour's walk from Souyia. It has Greek and Roman remains, most notably the temple to Asklepios, the god of healing. Also on the site are two thirteenth-century churches and some early tombs.

Souyia has a long, pebbly beach with caves at one end in which people set up camp for the summer. Overall, the village has a faintly odd atmosphere; it is neither a tourist resort nor a genuine local settlement. It does, however, seem popular with hippy travellers.

The best road to Paleohora is that which leaves the north coast at Tavronitis. Until Voukolies the road is wide and rapid but it soon turns into a typical, winding mountain drive in an uninhabited landscape.

**Floria**, near the halfway point, has two Byzantine churches (these are particularly widespread in this region) and a memorial in German and Greek to those killed in the war.

**Kandanos** is the biggest village in the area, but having been totally destroyed by the Germans, it is now completely modern. A large memorial in the square includes the original sign erected by the Germans which is in German and translates as, 'Here is Kandanos destroyed in retribution for the murder of 25 German soldiers'.

Beyond Kandanos is the Kakodiki region, famous for its many

## Places of Interest Inland From Hania and On the South Coast

**Theriso Gorge**
A narrow ravine through beautiful countryside.

**Lakki**
A picturesque mountain village, active in the resistance against the Germans.

**Omalos Plateau**
Unusual high plain, covered in snow in winter but fertile in summer and surrounded by high mountains.

**Samaria Gorge**
The longest gorge in Europe. Provides a 5 to 6 hour hike undertaken by huge numbers of visitors attracted by its dramatic scenery culminating in the Iron Gates, its narrowest point, with sheer rock walls only a few feet apart.

**Souyia**
A small, out of the way village with a long beach and a few rooms to rent.

*Lissos*
Site of an ancient temple to the god of healing, accessible only on foot and about 1 hour's walk from Souyia.

**Paleohora**
A growing resort with a sandy beach and lively port.
*Castel Selino*
A Venetian fortress which was restored after being destroyed in the sixteenth century by Barbarossa. It is open to the public.

old churches. **Kalithes** (Kallithea) is a particularly attractive village; it has floral gardens and is just a few kilometres away from Paleohora.

**Paleohora** is developing into a sizeable resort from its coastal village origins. It may have been the site of a Classical Greek town but the only certain period of its early history is that of the Venetians, who called it Castel Selino after the fortress they built there. Barbarossa mounted a pirate raid in 1539 which destroyed the fort, although it has been restored somewhat since then and is open to the public.

The village has several supermarkets, a bank, post office and telephone office, all on the single main road. Around the port are a large number of cafés and this is where boats leave for Elafonisi or Ayia Roumeli.

*The abandoned village of Samaria*

There is a beach beyond the harbour but the best beach is on the other side of the village. It is long, sandy and wide enough to be well away from the road but it can become crowded nearer the town.

One possible excursion from Paleohora is to the offshore island of Gavdhos. The boat trip takes about 4 hours and, apart from a few basic rooms, there is nothing else there. The beaches are unspoilt and ideal for visitors wishing to spend a few days isolated from the rest of the world. Local travel agents have details of the trip.

It is possible to drive across to Souyia from Paleohora or vice versa although not on the major highway marked on some maps. This has yet to be built and official signposts are both optimistic and premature.

The best route is to return to Kandanos and then take the road south into the hills signposted Bambakados and Temenia which is a pleasant drive through a lush valley. The road is tarmac until 1.5km (1 mile) away from Maza, when it becomes a dirt track. From Maza to Rodovani the road has short unpaved stretches which are interspersed with tarmac. From Rodovani it is an easy drive to Souyia. Other routes are possible but involve longer stretches of bad road.

# Tips for Travellers

## Planning Your Visit

## Basic Things to Pack

In major tourist resorts all medical supplies are easily obtainable but expensive. Away from these areas, imported goods are hard to obtain.

It is advisable to pack the following:-

**Mosquito repellent**
Mosquitoes, although not malaria carriers, can be a major irritation. It is advisable to take, or buy when you are there, electrically heated or tablet repellents as well as cream or lotion.

**Sun cream**
Visitors should take care in the sun especially in the first few days. Sun cream is more expensive on the island although widely available.

**Torch**
This would prove invaluable for exploring caves.

**Camera equipment**
Visitors should buy film in their home country. It is expensive in Crete and may have been stored in the sun for long periods. While on the island care should be taken to protect cameras from the heat; never leave cameras in a car parked in the sun.

**Clothes**
Spring and summer visitors will only need light clothes such as T shirts and shorts. Evenings are generally warm but a light pullover should be taken. Those wishing to make trips into the mountains such as the excursion to the Samaria Gorge should pack walking shoes, or good training shoes, rainwear and pullovers, especially in spring and autumn.

# Climate

Summer temperatures are often moderated by the strong north-westerly wind called the Meltemi which blows in July and August. The south of the island tends to be hotter and drier than the north. The mountains in the centre of the island serve as a block to rain. Therefore, bad weather in the south may leave the north fine or vice versa. The mountainous regions are always cooler and in winter can be covered in snow.

*Weather Information: Iraklion*

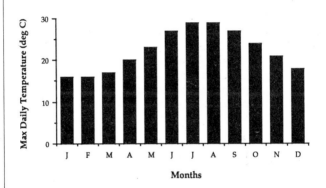

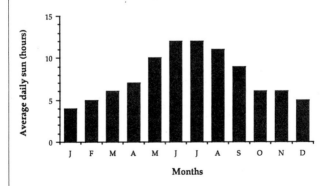

*Sunset*

| | |
|---|---|
| May | 8.05pm |
| June | 8.29pm |
| July | 8.38pm |
| August | 8.23pm |
| September | 7.46pm |
| October | 6.03pm |

*When to Go*

The best time to visit the island is in the spring, between April and June. The summer months are very hot; the landscape is dusty and plagued by strong winds.

## Currency and Credit Cards

The unit used is the Drachma (Dr) with 5, 10, 20 and 50 Drachmas and notes of 50, 100, 500, 1,000 and 5,000.

There is a limit of 3,000 Drachmas in notes that can be brought into the country. There are no restrictions on foreign money coming in as travellers cheques but large amounts, £300 or more, need to be declared if exported again. In practice, these regulations need only concern those wishing to work on the island and then take out their earnings.

There are banks in all major towns and resorts; the staff usually speak a little English although they do have a reputation for slow service.

**Opening hours:** Monday-Friday 8am-2pm occasionally later in major tourist centres. Some banks close at 1pm on Fridays.

Post offices also run an exchange service open Monday-Friday 8am-1.30pm and in the temporary yellow portakabins 8am-8pm; Sundays 9am-6pm. You may find the post offices offer a better exchange rate than the banks. Exchange facilities are also available in some travel agents, hotels and tourist offices; check the rates beforehand as these tend to be very unfavourable.

Commission is always charged and varies from bank to bank. There can be long queues at banks in major towns.

Eurocheques are accepted by banks but not shops. Major credit cards will probably be accepted by shops in the big resorts as well as by hire car firms, hotels and large restaurants but by no means universally. Visitors are unlikely to be able to use their credit cards in smaller resorts.

## Customs and Duty Free Allowances

*Duty Free Goods*
200 cigarettes or 50 cigars
1 litre of spirits
2 litres of 22% alcohol
2 litres of wine
50g ($1^3/_4$oz) of perfume

*Duty Paid Goods*
300 cigarettes or 75 cigars
1.5 litres of spirits
3 litres of 22% alcohol
5 litres of wine
75g ($2^1/_2$oz) of perfume
There are strict regulations prohibiting the export of antiquities and archaeological artefacts.

## Disabled Visitors

There are few facilities for disabled visitors on the island and they may encounter particular problems in airports and bus stations. Travellers with mobility problems need to research their trip carefully before hand, bearing in mind the mountainous terrain of the island and the poor state of the roads and pavements. The tourist offices have limited information and organisations in the visitor's home country may be of more help.

## Distances

Two factors should be borne in mind when planning
trips by car to outlying areas. Firstly, the shortest route
may not necessarily be the quickest; dirt roads are
unbearably slow and much longer, tarred routes will be
quicker. Secondly, the Cretans' inability to give accurate
estimates of distance or time between places is legendary, treat any such estimates with extreme scepticism,
they are almost certainly optimistic. It is also worth
bearing in mind that if you are staying in the south of the
island, it takes 1-2 hours to get to the towns on the north
coast. In the summer, this can leave the visitor feeling
exceedingly hot and tired.

Distances are given for the most direct route.

| Iraklion | |
|---|---|
| | to Ayia Galini 84km (52 miles) |
| | to Ayios Nikolaos 70km (43$^1/_2$ miles) |
| | to Hania 137km (85 miles) |
| | to *Knossos* 5km (3 miles) |
| | to Matala 75km (46$^1/_2$ miles) |
| | to *Phaestos* 60km (37 miles) |
| | to Rethimnon 78km (48 miles) |

| **Rethimnon** | to Ayia Galini 62km (38$^1/_2$ miles) |
| | to Hania 59km (36$^1/_2$ miles) |
| | to Hora Sfakion 70km (43$^1/_2$ miles) |

| **Hania** | to Kastelli Kissamou 43km (26$^1/_2$ miles) |
| | to Paleohora 77km (48 miles) |
| | to Souyia 70km (43$^1/_2$ miles) |

| **Ayios Nikolaos** | to Ierapetra 35km (22 miles) |
| | to Sitia 70km (43$^1/_2$ miles) |

## *Electric Current*

Voltage in Crete is 220 A/C. Two pin plugs are used, so an adaptor will be needed for British electrical appliances.

## *Health*

Under EEC regulations, an E111 form should provide treatment for UK residents while in Greece. American visitors should check that they are covered by their health insurance. The public health facilities are very limited. The only satisfactory option is to be treated privately, in which case treatment has to be paid for. It is therefore virtually essential to take out holiday insurance to cover medical emergencies. It is also important to check that holiday insurance covers the cost of being flown home urgently.

Although not obligatory, visitors might consider being vaccinated for typhoid and polio. Tap water, however, is safe to drink throughout the island.

Visitors should be aware of the health hazards of spending too long in the summer sun, especially when they first arrive on the island. Sun cream is therefore essential and it should be noted that sunburn is possible even on windy and cooler days.

There are English speaking doctors in most major

towns. Consulates may be able to give details.

Chemists operate a rota to provide 24 hour cover and the chemists themselves can usually advise on treatment for minor complaints. Visitors using a prescription drug should bring a copy of the prescription to avoid problems at customs. It should be noted that codeine, often found in headache pills, is banned in Greece.

Phone 166 for an ambulance, 171 for the tourist police, who usually speak English and will help in emergencies.

*Iraklion Hospital*
Venizelou Street
☎ 081 237580

*Hania Hospital*
Kopodistriou Street
☎ 0821 22222

*Ayios Nikolaos Hospital*
Lasithous Street
☎ 0841 27814

*Rethimnon Hospital*
Tranthadou Street
☎ 0831 27814

## *Language and Spelling*

Almost all Cretans speak some English or German and most signs, menus and other instructions are in English. A knowledge of the Greek alphabet may be of some help in deciphering street names and signs in the more remote places, although an English translation is given in towns and on most road signs.

## The Greek Alphabet
The Greek alphabet consists of 24 letters as follows:

| A | α | a as in apology |
|---|---|---|
| B | β | pronounced a v in victory |
| Γ | γ | y as in yes |
| Δ | δ | th as in then |
| E | ε | e as in red |
| Z | ζ | z as in zero |
| H | η | i as in ill |
| Θ | θ | th as in thin |
| I | ι | i as in ill |
| K | κ | k as in king |
| Λ | λ | l as in lot |
| M | μ | m as in mother |
| N | ν | n as in now |
| Ξ | ξ | ks as in rocks |
| O | o | o as in corporal |
| Π | π | p as in paper |
| P | ρ | r as in red |
| Σ | σ | s as in sister |
| T | τ | t as in tin |
| Y | υ | i as in ill |
| Φ | φ | f as in fat |
| X | χ | h as in hill (heavily aspirated) |
| Ψ | ψ | ps as in lips |
| Ω | ω | o as in oscar |

The translation from Greek to English can be idiosyncratic. While on menus this is simply comic, on signposts it can be misleading. As far as possible, this book has used the spelling of place names as found on signs on the island although these are not always consistent.

Visitors should be aware that 'CH', 'H', 'KH' and even 'X' can all stand for the same Greek sound, hence the numerous ways of spelling Hania (Chania, Khania, Xania). 'G' and 'Y' are also frequently interchanged, as are 'PH' and 'F'. Double letters, as in Malia or Mallia, Amnissos or Amnisos, are a problem, as are combinations of vowels.

Other difficulties arise with the different declensions and genders of the nouns which mean place names may end in 'io' or 'ion' and sometimes 'ii', depending on the context. Further confusion is possible because many places have the same name. There are numerous Kastellis and several Episkopis, to name but two. Many villages are named after their saint. The Greek word for saint is *Ayia* or *Ayios*, depending on the gender of the saint. This is sometimes written as *Agia/Agios* or more rarely *Hagia/Hagios*.

When map reading, note that a village may be in two halves, *Ano* and *Kato* meaning upper and lower respectively. *Odhos* means street, and *plateia* square. *Spilia* is the word for a cave and *moni* is often used to designate a monastery.

**Useful Words and Phrases**
Yes — *ne*
No — *óhi*
Please — *parakaló*
Thank You — *efharistó*
Hello — *yásoo*
Goodbye — *héreteh*
Good morning — *kaliméra*
Good afternoon — *kalispéra*
Good night — *kalinicta*
Today — *simera*
Tomorrow — *avrio*
Yesterday — *hthes*
Bank — *trapeza*
Bus — *leoforio*
Car — *aftokinito*
Where is… — *pou eené*
How much? — *poso kani*
Do you speak English? — *milate anglika?*
A room — *ena dhomátio*
**Days of the week**
Sunday — *kiriaki*
Monday — *theftera*

Tuesday — *triti*
Wednesday — *tetarti*
Thursday — *pempti*
Friday — *paraskevi*
Saturday — *savaton*

**Numbers**

1 — *ena*
2 — *thio*
3 — *tria*
4 — *tessera*
5 — *pente*
6 — *exi*
7 — *epta*
8 — *okto*
9 — *ennea*
10 — *theka*
20 — *eekosi*
100 — *ekato*
200 — *thiakosi*
500 — *pentakosi*
1,000 — *hiliee*

## *Official Regulations for Entry into Crete*

A British or American passport is all that is required to enter Crete and this permits a stay of 3 months. To stay longer, an extension needs to be obtained from the local police. US citizens do not need a visa but can only stay for 2 months.

The Greek government has warned that any visitor with a stamp in their passport from the Turkish Republic of North Cyprus will not be allowed into Greece. Passengers on charter flights are not permitted to make trips to Turkey from Greece.

## Photography

There are some restrictions on photography around the island. Taking pictures inside churches is usually forbidden; photography in museums is allowed on payment of a fee which is substantial for cameras on tripods. There is a large military zone near Hania at Souda Bay where repeated signs forbid photography. This is also the case near Ayia Galini.

Films are available on the island but it is much better to bring them from home where they will be cheaper and less likely to have been stored in the sun. Visitors should take extra care to avoid leaving film or cameras in the heat, especially in locked cars. Film processing is sometimes offered in the resorts. This is expensive and likely to be of poor quality.

## Public Holidays

1 and 6 January
25 March
1 May
15 August
28 October
25 and 26 December

There are also public holidays for Greek Easter. Banks, post offices and public buildings are closed on these days. Many shops stay open or close for only part of the day.

## Time

Greek summertime is 3 hours ahead of GMT, 2 hours ahead of BST. Clocks move forward on the last Sunday in March and back on the last Sunday in September.

## *Tipping*

Service is generally included on bills but tips are always appreciated.

## *Tourist Offices*

**United Kingdom**
195-7 Regent Street
London W1R 8DL
☎ 071 734 5997

**USA**
New York
645 Fifth Avenue
Olympic Tower
NY 10022
☎ 4215777

Los Angeles
611 West Sixth Street
Los Angeles
California 90017
☎ 6266696

**Greek Embassy (UK)**
1a Holland Park
London W11 37D
☎ 071 727 8040

**Greek Embassy (USA)**
2221 Masachusetts Avenue
Washington DC 20008
☎ 6673168

**Greek Consulate**
69 East 79th Street
New York, NY 10021
☎ 9885500

# How To Get There

## By Air

There are no scheduled flights to the island direct from the UK or USA so most visitors arrive on charter flights either as part of a package holiday or on a flight-only deal which is possible with most of the major travel companies. Visitors should bear in mind that many of these are night flights and can arrive on the island very early in the morning and depart at equally inconvenient times.

Flights are to Iraklion and less fequently to Hania and depart from almost all the regional airports in the UK. The journey takes about $3^{1}/_{2}$ hours. Regulations require that visitors on flights have accommodation, in practice this means the travel company will issue a voucher to cover this formality but, in reality, this is not intended to be used.

There are no direct flights from the US to Crete. However, there are scheduled flights to Athens from Los Angeles, San Fransisco and New York. Alternatively, visitors could fly to London and take a charter flight from there.

Olympic Airlines runs scheduled flights to the island from Athens, taking 45 minutes. These offer an alternative way of reaching the island, with up to eight flights a day at the height of summer. However, changing planes in Athens, which usually involves changing terminals, can be stressful.

Virtually all companies require passengers to confirm their return flight a few days before departure — check for specific instructions on the ticket. Given the vagaries of the telephone system, it is advisable to do this as soon as possible.

There is a new airport at Sitia but this currently receives only a few flights from Rhodes.

*Summary of Olympic flights to the island*

| Iraklion | From and to Athens | 7 daily |
| | From and to Rhodes | 1 daily |
| | From and to Mykonos | 1 daily |
| | From and to Santorini | 3 per week |
| | From and to Paros | 3 per week |
| | From and to Thessaloniki | 2 per week |
| | | |
| Hania | From and to Athens | 5 daily |
| | | |
| Sitia | From and to Rhodes | 4 per week |

*Airport Information*
Iraklion 4km (2$^1$/$_2$ miles) east of the city
☎ 081 282025

Hania 13km (8 miles) from the city at Sternes on the
Akrotiri Peninsula
☎ 0821 63264

*Olympic Airlines Offices*
*Iraklion*
Plateia Eleftherias
☎ 081 229191

*Hania*
88 Tzankaki
☎ 0821 27701

*Rethimnon*
6 Dhimitrikaki
☎ 0831 22257
Airline tickets are available at many travel agents on the
island.

*Iraklion Airport*
The airport is 4km (2$^1$/$_2$ miles) east of Iraklion city centre
and fairly easy to find, despite erratic signposting. It
clearly cannot cope with the number of visitors it
receives at the height of the season and this leads to

considerable delays in waiting for baggage. The four check-in desks are inadequate and queues usually form and stretch outside the door. Frequent announcements are made in both Greek and English and are usually quite clear but the information television screens often break down.

There are few facilities inside the airport other than a small souvenir shop, a restaurant upstairs and a small snack bar. The toilets are, however, remarkably clean.

All the major car hire firms have desks which are staffed from 7am to 11pm. Taxis are available and charges displayed on a board inside the check-in area. Package tours are usually met by coach. There is a scheduled bus to and from Iraklion leaving from outside the tourist office every 10 minutes until 11pm. It stops on the main road about 700m (2,300ft) away from the airport. Olympic Airlines run a bus to the airport to meet their frequent flights. These leave from their office in Plateia Eleftherias.

## By Sea

Most ferries come to the island from Piraeus although there are some boats from the other Greek islands, including Rhodes.
There are two ferries a day to Iraklion from Piraeus and one to Hania, both trips take 12 hours and run through the night, leaving Piraeus in the early evening.

There is a daily service from Thera (Santorini) to Iraklion; three ferries a week to Naxos and Ios and less frequent services from the other islands.

Twice weekly ferries from Rhodes and Piraeus call at Ayios Nikolaos and Sitia.

There are also weekly services from Limassol (Cyprus) and Haifa (Israel). A hydrofoil service runs from Iraklion to the Cyclades. Ferries have four classes of accommodation; first, second, tourist and deck, with differing prices to match. In summer these boats can be crowded and cabins very hot. Facilities are far from luxurious.

*Ferry Offices*
There are two ferry companies running the Athens
service; Anek and Minoan.

*Iraklion*
Minoan
78 Odhos 25 Avgostou
☎ 081 229602

Anek
Odhos 25 Avgostou
☎ 081 222481

*Hania*
Minoan
c/o Nanadakis Travel
8 Halidhon
☎ 0821 22939/24352

Anek
Plateia Sophia
Venizelou
☎ 0821 23636/51915

Ferry tickets are also available from any travel agents.
Alternative ways of reaching the island include the train
or taking the coach across Europe. These journeys, while
significantly cheaper than air travel, can be extremely
tiring and stressful.


## When You Are There

## Dress Regulations

Visitors will not be allowed into religious buildings
unless 'properly dressed' ie no shorts or bare shoulders.

## Laws for Children

There are no restrictions on children visiting monuments or churches.

## Motoring

Drivers taking their own car to the island should consult a motoring organisation and the Greek tourist office for details of insurance requirements and other regulations. A green card is necessary and it is compulsory to carry a first-aid kit, a warning triangle and a fire extinguisher in the car.

Driving is on the right and British or American driving licences are usually acceptable. Road signs follow the standard international format.

It is important to be prepared for the reckless driving of some of the locals and the additional hazards of goats and donkeys, which have right of way on the roads.

The screenwash should be checked regularly for the summer dust can often cover the screen. Visitors should be aware that cars left parked in the sun can become unbearably hot and, wherever possible, they should park in the shade.

Apart from the new coastal highway, roads in Crete are not good, being littered with potholes, prone to subsidence and, in the mountains very narrow and subject to rock falls.

Although many roads nowadays are asphalted, several places of interest are still only accessible on dirt tracks and care should be taken on these as no hire car company insures the underside or tyres of the car. Even fast tarmac roads can peter out without warning into dirt tracks. When planning routes, drivers should bear in mind that it will often be quicker to take a long detour on asphalted roads rather than travel even a short distance on a dirt track. The latter will always be painfully slow.

As villagers have to pay for the upkeep of the sections of road within their village, these are usually in a terrible state of repair and extra caution is required on these surfaces, especially in bad weather.

**Car Hire**
Cars are available for hire in most resorts on the island and at the airports. No company will hire to those under 21 and some have an age limit of 25; paying by credit card seems to allow some relaxation of these age limits. Check what is being offered in the deal; the nature of the insurance and if a collision damage waiver is included, without this the driver has to pay for damage which is his or her fault.

Cars are sometimes sent out in poor condition and it is advisable to check whether there is a jack and the state of the spare tyre before accepting a car.

Mopeds are also widely available for hire. Crash helmets are not automatically available but, bearing in mind the mountainous terrain and the state of the roads, these are highly recommended. Numerous severe accidents happen every year to tourists hiring these vehicles. See also the section on Driving Regulations.

# Emergencies

### Accidents
In case of serious accidents, contact your consul. In all cases record all details; take a photograph of the scene if possible. Do not make any statements unless they are being recorded by someone who speaks fluent English. The tourist police will help in such cases.

### Breakdowns
Hire car companies have their own procedures which usually involve a phone number to contact.

As far as those driving their own car are concerned, the AA and RAC have reciprocal agreements with their Greek equivalent ELPA, who will give assistance to members while in Greece. Contact your motoring organisation for details.

### Fuel

There are filling stations in all but the most remote areas and these are open long hours; at least 7am-7pm, with many in towns and resorts open on Sundays as well. Most hire cars take 'super'. There are very few self service stations and currently only a very few selling lead free petrol. The latter include stations in Iraklion and Hania and one on the new Iraklion to Ayios Nikolaos road near Hersonissos.

### Motoring Regulations

Speed limits are 100kmh (62mph) on national highways, ie north coast road; lorries and mopeds 70kmh (43mph). Other roads outside towns have a limit of 70kmh (43mph). Within towns the limit is 40kmh (25mph). Other limits are indicated locally. Use of seat belts is compulsory in the front of the car.

### Signposts

Signposts are reasonably good in most areas. Usually there is a sign in Greek followed by an English translation 50m (55yd) further on, often just in from the turning. Specific sites tend to be well-signposted at first but further forks and turns often lack any marking.

Confusion may also arise with the existence of new road (*nea odhos*) and old road (*palea odhos*) signs; drivers should establish not only their destination but also which route they wish to take.

## *Police*

The police are generally felt to be friendly towards foreigners although visitors who are deemed to be undesirable may find themselves unwelcome. Young people sleeping on the beach may well be asked to move on and it is best to comply with this regulation.

Until recently, there was a special branch of the police which dealt with tourists and were connected to the tourist offices. However, these sections are slowly being amalgamated back into the ordinary police force and based at police stations. If you have anything stolen, contact the police or tourist police and register the loss for insurance claims.

Generally, there is very little crime on the island. The limited amount of trouble tends to be caused by overseas visitors.

In any encounter with the police, it is always advisable to wait until someone who speaks fluent English arrives on the scene. In the event of a serious difficulty, the consulate should be contacted to help find a lawyer.

**Legal Advice**
The relevant consulate will arrange for a lawyer but cannot do much more than this.

# Post

Post offices can be found in all major towns and in resorts there are supplementary caravans painted bright yellow.

Normal opening hours are 8am-8pm Monday-Friday in large centres but in smaller towns offices may close in the early afternoon. Post offices will also exchange money. Stamps (*gramatosima*) can also be bought at many souvenir shops but will be slightly more expensive than from the post office. Letter boxes are bright yellow and have a horn symbol marked on them.

# Public Toilets

There are few public toilets. They are generally dirty and you should take your own toilet paper. Toilets in tavernas and museums are marginally better.

# Public Transport

**Bus Services**

Although travelling by car is the most convenient way to see the island, there is an extensive bus network which is widely used by visitors. There are main bus stations in Ayios Nikolaos, Iraklion, Hania and Rethimnon and buses between these towns are frequent. There are also services to the sites at *Knossos* and *Phaestos* as well as the Samaria Gorge.

The service is run by KTEL which is a grouping of several companies, each covering a particular region. This may cause complications on longer journeys and explains the need for several bus stations in the main towns. There are four in Iraklion; visitors arriving from the east use the bus station by the ferry port; those from the west use that on the seafront near the Historical Museum; the station just outside the Hania Gate serves the south-west, and buses heading for the south-east of the island (Ierapetra) arrive at a small bus station at the far end of Odhos Evans just outside the walls.

Trips to smaller villages may be difficult. Although there is usually a bus service, these are run for the benefit of villagers who wish to come into town in the morning and return in the evening, whereas tourists wish to journey in the opposite direction.

Timetables and prices are available from the local tourist information offices. Tickets can be bought at bus stations and on the buses themselves.

**Taxis**

Taxis are reasonably cheap, especially if shared, and present the only way of reaching some of the more remote areas. It is always worth checking the fare before you start.

*Alternative Travel*

Numerous excursions are offered by the travel agents on the island; these include visits to the major sites and beaches, as well as trips to see local culture and folklore in the mountain villages. Obviously, these follow well-beaten tourist circuits.

## Religion

Greek Orthodox

## Shops

Food shops tend to be small and multi-purpose although rarely selling bread. There are bakeries in virtually all towns but these are often hidden in side streets. Many of the mountain villages have no shops at all and it is advisable to stock up before heading into remote areas.

Opening hours tend to depend on the location of the shop; in resorts the shops are open until very late at night everyday including Sunday. Smaller places tend to open 8am-1pm and then close for siesta until 4pm or 5pm then staying open until 8pm, but these are general guidelines and hours can vary considerably.

In all resorts there are a wide range of souvenir shops although it has to be said that much of what they sell is of poor quality. Genuine local craft shops are worth seeking out and make a change from the cheap imitation souvenirs. Generally, the shops which have a captive tourist market have more expensive and less attractive goods. The small side streets in Hania and Rethimnon are the best places to find local craftsmen at work.

Village shops do not sell a wide range of goods but in the towns it should be possible to find all that a visitor might need although products like toiletries and other imported goods will be more expensive than at home.

### Things to Buy
Local pottery; often very fine, hand-crafted goods. Hand-woven cloth; avoid the more obviously tourist-oriented villages where quality can be poor and goods expensive.

Sponges; natural sponges are sold in many resorts often from makeshift stalls.

Olives and olive oil; the staple crop of the island and widely available in tins and jars.

## *Taboo Subjects*

Greece is now a democracy and less politically volatile than before but extolling the virtues of Turkey is likely to receive a frosty reception.

## *Telephones*

There are telephone boxes in most towns, the ones with the orange band are for international calls. The largest coin they can take is 20 Drachmas. Furthermore, they rarely work and these two factors combined mean that making long-distance calls from these boxes is virtually impossible.

The alternative is to find an OTE office where there are metred phones. You make your call and then pay at the desk afterwards. There are main offices in large towns and in resorts smaller temporary offices. In large towns these are open 7am-10pm and sometimes longer. However, in smaller places these offices often close at 3.30pm. Staff generally speak a little English and are usually helpful. Some tourist shops also offer this service.

The code for the United Kingdom is 00 44 leaving off the zero of the STD code. For the USA the code is 001. To ring Crete from the UK dial 01030.

The ringing tone is a long repeated sound; the engaged one is a shorter, staccato tone.

It should be noted that it is usually very difficult to get an international connection and it maybe necessary to dial more than a dozen times before getting through, there is no other option than persistence. It may be easier, if more expensive, to ask your hotel to connect you.

There are various local codes for calls within the island:
Iraklion 081
Hania 0821
Rethimnon 0831
Ayios Nikolaos 0841
Sitia 0843
Kastelli Kisamou 0822
Ierapetra 0842

**Useful Numbers**
100 Emergencies
166 Ambulance
171 Police
151 Operator
161 International operator
131 Local directory enquiries
01 169 International directory enquiries

# FURTHER INFORMATION FOR VISITORS

## Accommodation

Most visitors to the island come with pre-booked hotel or apartment accommodation. However, there are ample facilities for the independent traveller in the form of rooms to rent, either in private houses or more usually above a taverna or in a purpose-built block. Rooms are available in almost every town and village on the island and advertised in English as 'Rent Rooms' or 'Pensions'. The only places where it may be diffcult to find rooms are in the newer resorts which cater purely for package tourists.

There are three categories of room; the category and price should be displayed in Greek and English on the back of the door. Local taxes may be added to this price and sometimes showers are extra. Out of season, the price charged may be lower than that displayed. Generally, proprietors accept visitors for any length of stay, although those staying more than one night may benefit from a favourable rate. It is customary to be shown the room before making

any decision to accept it.

The *alpha* category usually means the room has an en suite bathroom, *beta* a sink in the room and *gamma* a room where all washing facilities are shared with the other residents. Rooms are generally very good value; they tend to be neater and cleaner than hotels. In fact, there are very few hotel rooms available in summer as most are block booked by travel companies.

It is normal practice for the proprietors of rooms to keep a passport which is returned on departure.

When selecting a room it is advisable to bear in mind that those in or near tavernas will be noisy until the early hours of the morning.

It should be noted that the Greek plumbing system uses narrower pipes than other European countries and, to avoid blockages, toilet paper should be placed in the bin provided. Hot water can be another problem, sometimes the taps have been put on the wrong way round, sometimes there is simply an erratic supply. Visitors may be surprised that there is no separate shower unit, the shower is fixed to the bathroom wall and the water is supposed to drain away through the hole in the floor. A brush is sometimes provided to assist in the drainage process.

Some rooms provide a communal fridge for residents' use. Very occasionally, there are cooking facilities.

Tourist offices provide comprehensive lists of hotels (not rooms) in their brochures and may be able to help with accommodation although, in practice, it is only at the real height of the season that there will be any shortage of places and even then only in the major resorts.

## Archaeological Sites

Archaeological sites fall into three categories:
1 Much visited sites like *Knossos* which charge admission fees and have fixed opening hours.
2 Fenced sites with a warden but free admission and open daylight hours.
3 Unfenced sites with free access.

Summer opening hours are given, out of season hours may be restricted.

### Aptera
Near Hania
Classical site
Unfenced site, open during the day.

### Ayia Triadha
3km (2 miles) from *Phaestos*
Minoan villa
Open: Monday to Thursday and Saturday 8.45am-3.30pm, closed Friday. Sunday 9.30am-2.30pm.
Admission charge.

### Dreros
Near Neapolis
Classical site.
Unfenced site.

### Gortyn
Outside Ayia Deka
Roman site, postcard shop.
Open: Every day 8am-7pm.
Admission charge.
Other ruins are scattered across the road, freely accessible.

### Gournia
18km (11 miles) east of Ayios Nikolaos
Minoan town.
Fenced site, free admission, open during the day.

### Knossos
5km (3 miles) south of Iraklion
Minoan palace; bookshop.
Open: 8am-7pm daily.
Admission charge.

### Lato
10km (6 miles) inland from Ayios Nikolaos
Doric city.
Unfenced site.

### Malia
2km (1 mile) from modern town
Minoan palace; postcard shop.
Open: Monday to Saturday

8.45am-1.00pm. Sunday 9.30am-2.30pm.
Admission charge.

*Phaestos*
Between Timbaki and Mires
Minoan palace; tourist pavilion.
Open: Monday to Saturday 8am-7pm. Sunday 9am-6pm.
Admission charge.

*Tilissos*
13km (8 miles) south of Iraklion
Minoan villas.
Open: Tuesday to Saturday
8.45am-3pm. Sunday 9.30am-2.30pm. Closed Monday.
Admission charge.

*Zakros*
South of Paleokastro
Minoan Palace
Open: Everyday 9am-5pm.
Admission charge.

# *Archaeological Terms*

**Achaens**   Name of Classical Greek people in Homeric times, also known as Myceneans.

**Agora**   Market place or public meeting place.

**Central Court**   Paved area at the centre of Minoan palaces probably used for ceremonies and games.

**Eteocretans**   The last of the Minoans who took to the hills after the catastrophe in 1450BC.

**Faience**   Quartz substance covered in a layer of glass used in jewellery and vases.

**Frescoes**   Wall paintings found in the palaces, often naturalistic scenes in bright colours.

**Gypsum**   Pinkish stone used extensively by the Minoans.

**Labyrinth**   Maze of the Minotaur legend.

**Larnakes**   Clay burial coffins often in the shape of bathtubs.

**Linear A and B Script**   Early hieroglyphic form of writing. Linear B has been deciphered and is a form of Greek.

**Lustral Basin**   Small sunken rooms for ritual anointing.

**Megaron**   Royal room or hall in a Minoan palace.

**Minoan**   Name given to the Bronze Age people of Crete and the period in which they lived. This is then divided into Early Minoan, Middle Minoan and Late Minoan.

**Peak Sanctuaries**   Places of worship and shrines on mountain peaks or caves.

**Pithoi**   Huge storage jars used by the Minoans but still in use today.

**Rhyton**   A specially designed vessel for pouring libations.

**Tholos Tomb**   A circular tomb usually for a whole family.

## *Beaches*

Most beaches on the island are simply that; sand and sea with no other facilities except, perhaps, a taverna. Water sports are widely available, especially in major resorts, but these facilities vary from year to year. Umbrellas and deck chairs may also be available but only on very popular beaches.

Surfaces range from golden sand to grey shingle and this too can change from year to year depending on the ferocity of the winter storms. The sea is usually safe although every year there are a few cases of tourists drowning and none of the beaches have life-guards. Extra care should be taken on windy days when the sea can be quite rough and strong currents are created.

Topless bathing is widespread on all beaches although it does offend the older generation of Cretans. Naturism is expressly forbidden on many beaches but there are numerous secluded coves where nudists are tolerated. However, a certain amount of discretion is still advisable.

Beaches in the major resorts are often crowded during the summer. At weekends the local population tends to go to the beach and this can make certain places, which are deserted during the week, very busy.

**Almyrida**
Sandy beach, water sports.

**Amnissos**
Beach close to the airport.
Tavernas.

**Amoudhara**
Sandy beach close to holiday development.

**Arvi**
Beach near the village.

**Ayia Galini**
Beach near resort.
All facilities.

**Ayia Pelayia**
Beach by restaurants.

**Bali**
Three coves.
Water sports, tavernas.

**Elafonisi**
Isolated beach.
Boat trips possible from Paleohora.

**Falasarna**
Sandy beach and tavernas.

**Georgioupolis**
Long, sandy beach near village.

**Gerani**
Rocky beach.

**Hania**
Beach west of the town.

**Hersonissos**
Resort beach.
All facilities.

**Ierapetra**
Town beach.
Water sports, tavernas, umbrellas for hire.

**Itanos**
Small sandy beach.

**Kalives**
Town beach.

**Kastelli**
Town beach.

**Kolimvari**
Tavernas and pebbly beach.

**Kokkino Pirgos**
Sandy beach, tavernas, shower.

**Lendas**
Beach by village and also beyond cape.
Tavernas.
Beach beyond cape permits naturism.

**Makrigialos**
Fine sandy beach.
Some water sports.

**Malia**
Resort beach.
All facilities; small offshore island.

**Matala**
Sandy beach by town; umbrellas.
Campsite adjacent to the beach.
Cafés at edge of it.
Red and Kommos Beaches beyond the village permit naturism.

**Mirtos**
Beach and restaurants.

**Mohlos**
Beach and offshore island with historical site. Nearby village.

**Pachia Amnos**
Long, sandy beach with tavernas.

**Paleohora**
South coast beach, water sports.

**Panormos**
Village beach.

**Plaka**
Pebbly beach.

**Plakias**
Long, sandy beach by small village.

**Platanias**
Beach with water sports and tavernas.

**Preveli**
Isolated beach with lagoon.

**Rethimnon**
Town beach.
Umbrellas, water sports, cafés nearby.

**Sitia**
Beach close to the town.

**Souyia**
Beach, shower.

**Stavros**
Beach and taverna.

**Vai**
Palm beach and taverna.
Car park and toilets.

**Zakros** (Kato)
Beach and taverna.

# Books and Maps

There are numerous books dealing with the archaeology of Crete, the main reference works still being those by the British archaeologists who excavated *Knossos* and lived on the island.

Arthur Evans, *The Palace of Minos*
J.S. Pendlebury, *The Archaeology of Crete*

Other detailed and scholarly studies include;
C. Davaras, *Guide to Cretan Antiquities*
R.W. Hutchinson, *Prehistoric Crete*
RF Willets, *The Civilisation of Ancient Crete*

There are few books dealing with the more recent history of the island with the exception of the events of the Battle of Crete during World War II. There are numerous works on this subject, ranging from military history to more personal accounts.

George Psychoundakis, *The Cretan Runner*, a local's account of the Cretan resistance.
Alan Clark *The Fall of Crete*, a military history of the battle.
W.Stanley Moss *Ill met by Moonlight*, an account of the kidnapping of General Kreipe.

All the above are available in cheap local editions on the island.
Kazantzakis is the only Cretan fiction writer of any international repute. His works have recently been reissued and include: *Zorba the Greek; The Last Temptation of Christ* and *Freedom and Death*, the latter being an account of a revolt against the Turks.

More recent times are dealt with in *Winds of Crete*, an account of an American, David MacNeil Doren's years on the island. A good general history of the island is Adam Hopkins' *Crete, Its Past, Present and People*.

A limited selection of books in English are available in major towns and resorts, although books published in England are very expensive. Local editions relating to Greece and Crete are cheaper.

English newspapers are widely available a day late.

## Maps
Maps of the island are notoriously inaccurate, especially those issued by the hire car companies. The Clyde Leisure map seems to be the best option for tourists. It is cheaper and more widely available in Britain than on Crete.

# Campsites

Camping on unrecognised sites is officially forbidden but on isolated beaches it is usually tolerated. Official sites have few facilities other than a taverna probably run by the owner of the site.

**Arcadia**
5km (3 miles) east of Rethimnon
250 places
☎ 0831 28746/24693

**Ayia Galini**
Ayia Galini
45 places
☎ 0832 91239/91386

**Ayia Marina**
9km (5$^1/_2$ miles) west of Hania,
Ayia Marina Beach
80 places
☎ 0821 68555

**Creta Camping**
Gouves, 20km (12$^1/_2$ miles) east of
Iraklion
90 places
☎ 0897 41400

**Elizabeth**
5km (3 miles) east of Rethimnon
164 places
☎ 0831 28694

**Gournia Moon**
Pachia Amnos, 15km (9 miles) east
of Ayios Nikolaos
55 places
☎ 0842 93243

**Ierapetra**
Ayii Saranta Beach, east of
Ierapetra
41 places
☎ 0842 22739/61351

**Iraklion**
Amoudhara Beach 7km (4 miles)
west of Iraklion
283 places
Swimming pool
☎ 081 286380/250986

**Koutsounari**
Roussa Skala Beach, Ierapetra
66 places
☎ 0842 61213

**Matala**
Matala Beach

**Mithymna**
37km (23 miles) west of Hania;
Drapanias
34 places
☎ 0822 31444

**Paleohora**
Paleohora town
34 places
☎ 0823 41225

**Sisi Camping**
Sisi
107 places
☎ 081 281444

## Caves

There are over 2,000 caves on the
island, many of them important
archaeological and historical sites.
Visitors should note that none of
the caves on the island are lit and a
powerful torch is invaluable. The
caves can be steep and slippery so
sensible shoes should be worn for
any exploration. Special permission
to visit those which are closed for
excavation work may be obtained
through the tourist office. Visitors
should check in any case before
visiting the caves, as the situation
concerning access may change.

**Eileithyia Cave**
Near Amnissos
Ancient remains.
Closed to the public.

### Idaiean Cave
15 minute walk beyond the tourist pavilion
Claimed to be legendary birthplace of Zeus.
Closed to the public.

### Kamares Cave
4 hours walk from Kamares
Ancient remains.
Open to the public.

### Melidoni Cave
1km ($^1/_2$ mile) from Melidoni
Memorial altar to those asphyxiated here by the Turks.
Open to the public.

### Psychro Cave
1km ($^1/_2$ mile) from Psychro
Birthplace of Zeus.
Open to the public, guides and mules available.

## Children

The Greeks have a reputation for spoiling their children and as a result children are welcomed in every establishment on the island. There are, however, few specific organised activities for their needs. On beaches etc they will have to amuse themselves. The sea is generally safe for children.

## Churches, Monasteries and Other Religious Buildings

Virtually all religious buildings on the island request that visitors are properly dressed ie no shorts or bare shoulders. Many monasteries are closed for siesta in the early afternoon.

### Arkhadi Monastery
23km (14 miles) south-east of Rethimnon
Monastery church; small museum, tourist pavilion.

### Ayia Ekaterini
Plateia Ayia Ekaterini, Iraklion
Museum of religious art and icons.
Open: Monday, Wednesday 9am-1pm. Tuesday, Thursday, Saturday 5pm-7pm. Closed Sunday.

### Ayios Titos
Plateia Titos, Iraklion
Church, skull of St Titus
Open: everyday.

### Gonia Monastery
1km ($^1/_2$ mile) beyond Kolimvari
Monastery church, small museum.
Closed 12.30-4.30pm for siesta.

### Gouverneto Monastery
Akrotiri Peninsula
Monastery and church.

### Hrissokalitissa Monastery
Far west of the island
Church.

**Kapsi Monastery**
East of Ierapetra
Monastery church.

**Panayia Kera**
10km (6 miles) north of Ayios
Nikolaos
Byzantine church; café, souvenir
shop.
Open: Monday to Saturday 9am-
3.15pm, Sunday 9am-2pm. Closed
Friday.

**Preveli Monastery**
Near Plakias
Monastery and nearby beach.

**Toplou Monastery**
16km (10 miles) east of Sitia
Monastery church, café outside,
postcard shop.
Closed for siesta 2pm-5pm.

**Vrondisi Monastery**
21km (13 miles) from Ayia Varvara
Monastery church
Open: all day.

There are modern cathedrals in
Hania, Iraklion and Rethimnon.
Hania and Rethimnon both have
numerous mosques; in Rethimnon
the Nerantzes Djani Minaret is
open to the public.

There are a large number of
Byzantine churches in all parts of
the islands. These are usually in the
smaller villages and often contain
fine frescoes. They are often locked
and it can be difficult to get the
key, the best place to ask is at the
local café.

## Entertainment

In the holiday resorts there are
large numbers of bars, discos and
clubs. There are usually organised
trips to see evenings of local
dancing or a bar in the resort may
specialise in local music.

There are cinemas in all major
towns; many of these are open-air.
The films are generally subtitled
rather than dubbed and so visitors
can consider the cinema as a
possible entertainment option.

Cultural festivals are held in
Iraklion, Ayios Nikolaos and some
other towns throughout the
summer. (See the section on Local
Events and Festivals).

## Food and Drink

The food offered in Crete restaurants can seem to lack variety. It
consists mainly of lamb or pork
and more often than not is served
with a few chips. Furthermore, the
extensive printed menus do not
represent the true extent of the
food on offer. Be prepared to be
told that one's initial choice is out
of season or simply not available.
This is not to say that is impossible
to have a good meal. Many
restaurants in the resorts do
provide extensive menus and good
food.

There are numerous Greek
equivalents of fast food sold from
roadside stalls. The fare includes
*souvlaki* and *gyros* ( meat in pitta

bread to take away).

The distinction between a taverna and a restaurant has virtually disappeared and both tend to offer the same type of food.

The best way to start a meal is probably a Greek salad, the contents of which vary but usually include tomato, cucumber and Feta cheese. Other starters include *taramosalata*, (smoked cod's roe presented as a kind of dip) or *tzatsiki* (yoghurt and cucumber).

Main courses include:
*Souvlaki*; pieces of pork or lamb served on skewers and barbecued, available in restaurants as a meal or from stalls as a snack.
*Kleftiko*: large pieces of roast lamb.
*Moussaka*; a mince dish topped with aubergines.
*Stifado*; a spicy stew.

Pork and lamb chops are common as is chicken and, more surprisingly, veal.

A variety of vegetables (tomatoes, aubergines) stuffed with mince and rice are a common dish. Meatballs also appear on many menus.

Fish is widely available, particularly squid (*kalamares*), red mullet (*barbounia*) and swordfish. Other varieties are sold by weight and are more expensive. This is true of lobster which is often on the menu and visible in many of the restaurants' display cabinets.

Bread is charged as an extra although it is always provided.

Desserts can be disappointing, usually consisting either of *baklava*, (an incredibly sweet cake) or

yoghurt with honey. In some of the resorts fruit salads and ice creams are available.

Cretan wine is generally felt to be reasonable in quality. *Retsina* is the cheapest available, although this resinated wine is something of an acquired taste and Kingsley Amis claimed, rather unkindly, that it tasted of 'stewed cricket bats'. *Ouzo* is another common drink, tasting of aniseed. *Raki* is the local strong spirit although it is not that widely available in restaurants.

As for soft drinks, lemonade is just that; a fizzy lemon drink, to get the lemonade foreigners are more used to, ask for 7Up or Sprite. Cans of drink are widely available in shops or kiosks and usually kept cool.

Coffee, unless otherwise specified, is what visitors will know as Turkish coffee although it would be tactless to use this name. It is very strong, sweet and served in a tiny cup.

In the more out of the way places, service can be very slow, it seems to be the local custom to leave clients to contemplate at length before taking their order. Eating out remains reasonably cheap although the non-local dishes can push the price up. If two prices are shown on the menu, it is the higher price which will be charged, this includes local taxes. Service is included but tips are always welcomed.

In all resorts, restaurants offer 'English Breakfast' in all its variations.

Every village on the island seems to have a *kafeinon*, the general meeting place of the village. These are open all day, mainly for coffee drinking, and are an exclusively male preserve. Roadside cafés are much more amenable to tourists and sell a wider range of drinks and sometimes ice cream.

Vegetarian food is not widely available and there is little variety of meat on sale, ie lamb, pork, chicken but little else. Tourist supermarkets stock a wide range of imported foodstuffs, although nothing exotic. Village shops have a limited variety of goods but have plenty of fruit and vegetables. Indeed, enormous varieties of fruit are on sale ranging from oranges to bananas, peaches and nectarines, depending on the season. Fruit is usually very good value. The system in most shops is that the customer fills a bag with his or her required selection and then has this weighed. Melons are abundant, especially in summer, and water melons are often sold at the side of the road.

The cheese pie is a local speciality sold from bakeries which will also sell all kinds of bread very cheaply; bread is usually not available in supermarkets. There are numerous cake shops in larger towns which sell fairly sweet, richly decorated, custard based cakes that make a filling snack. Ice creams tend to be pre-packaged and are rather expensive.

# *Local Events and Festivals*

Saints' days are very important in Crete and celebrated if a saint is associated with a particular village and by those bearing the name of that saint eg; all those named George and all villages with Ayios Yeorgios Church will celebrate on 23 April. These name days are usually more important than birthdays to those individuals concerned.

There are also various movable celebrations of dates in the Greek Orthodox calendar. Easter is usually on a different date to the western Easter and is a particularly important festival. It is accompanied by much feasting after the privations of Lent.

**Epiphany**; marked by the throwing of a cross into the sea.

**Clean Monday**; the beginning of Lent, celebrated with feasting.

**Independence Day**; 25 March; parades in major towns.

**Sheep shearing festival**; 23 April held in Asigonia.

**May Day**; picnics in the country.

**Battle of Crete Week**; in Hania 20-27 May.

**Naval Week**; displays and fireworks at the end of June.

**Rethimnon Wine Festival**; in the Public Gardens at the end of July.

**Ayios Titos Saints Day**; celebrated in Iraklion 25 August.

**Ayios Ioannis**; 29 August. The saints day marked with a pilgrimage to the monastery on the Rodopou Peninsula.

**Sitia Sultana Festival**; to celebrate the harvest; end of August.

**Elos Chestnut Festival**; to celebrate the harvest; October.

**Ohi Day**; national holiday in the Greek world to celebrate saying no, (*ohi*), to Mussolini; 28th October.

**Arkhadi Day**; on the anniversary of the explosion at the monastery, 7-9 November.

In addition to these fixed one day festivals, almost all the major towns hold summer festivals; the biggest of these is in Iraklion. During June, July, August and September there are cultural events all around the city, ranging from ballet by internationally known companies to recitals by local school choirs. Ayios Nikolaos and Ierapetra offer similar events on a smaller scale. Festival performances often take place in historic buildings or in the open air.

## *Museums*

**Ayios Nikolaos Archaeological Museum**
Odhos Palaiologou
Museum and bookshop.
Open: Monday to Saturday 8.45am-3pm. Sundays 9.30am-2pm.

Closed Tuesday.
☎ 0841 22462

**Ayios Yeoryios Folklore Museum**
Ayios Yeoryios, Lasithi.
Open: Monday to Sunday 10am-4pm.

**Hania Archaeological Museum**
Odhos Halidon
Open: Monday 12.30-7pm.
Tuesday to Friday 8am-7pm,
Saturday, Sunday 8am-3pm.
☎ 0821 24418

**Hania Historical Museum and City Archives**
20 Odhos Sphakianaki
☎ 0821 22600
Open: Monday to Friday 9am-1pm.
Closed weekends.

**Hania Naval Museum**
Firka Tower
Open: Tuesday, Thursday, Saturday 10am-2pm. Wednesday, Friday, Sunday 10am-2pm and 5-7pm.
Closed Monday.
☎ 0821 26437

**Ierapetra Archaeological Museum**
Adr. Kostoula Street
Open: 9am-3pm.
Closed Monday.

**Iraklion Archaeological Museum**
Plateia Eleftherias
Museum, bookshop, café.
Open: Tuesday to Saturday 8am-7pm. Sunday 9am-7pm.
Closed Monday.
☎ 081 226092

**Iraklion Historical Museum**
Sophocles Venizelou Street
Open: Monday to Saturday 9am-
1pm and 3-5.30pm.
Closed Sunday.
☎ 081 283219

**Ayia Ekaterini Icon Museum**
(Iraklion)
Plateia Ekaterini
Open: Monday, Wednesday,
Friday 9am-1pm. Tuesday,
Thursday, Saturday 9am-1pm and
5-7pm.
Closed Sunday.

**Kazantzakis Museum**
Mirtia village
Open: March to October. Monday,
Wednesday, Saturday, Sunday
9am-1pm and 4pm-8pm. Tuesday
and Friday 9am-1pm.
Closed Thursday.

**Sitia Archaeological Museum**
Lithines road
Open: Monday to Saturday 9am-
3pm. Sunday 9.30am-2.30pm.
Closed Tuesday.

The archaeological museums in
Rethimnon and Ierapetra are
currently closed.

## Mountaineering

**Refuges**
Levka Ori Kalergi (Hania) 1,680m
(5,510ft)
40 places
☎ 0821 24647

Levka Ori Volikas (Hania) 1,480m
(4,854ft)
30 places
☎ 0821 24647

Psiloritis Prinos 1,100m (3,608ft)
16 places
☎ 081 227609

Further information is available
from the Greek Alpine club;
74 Dhikeosinis Iraklion or
143 Arkhadiou; Rethimnon or
3 Mihelidhaki; Hania.
      There are numerous possibili-
ties for walks on the island
although there are very few
marked paths and no map
generally available showing
detailed information for walkers.
Local villagers are probably the
best source of information on the
surrounding area and may be
prepared to serve as guides. Also
recommended is *Crete: Off the
Beaten Track* by B. and N. Caughey,
published by Cicerone Press. The
book highlights country walks and
mountain hikes.

## Walking

The best areas for walkers are:
Coastal walks from Hora Sfakion to
Ayia Roumeli passing through
Loutro, Anopoli or Aradena.
      Walks on the tracks leading
from Kritsa village near Ayios
Nikolaos.
      Walks in the Psiloritis Range
from the tourist pavilion on the
Nidha Plateau. From here the

summit of Mount Ida can be tackled, this is also accessible from Kamares and Fourfouras.

Climbs in the Levka Ori starting from the Omalos Plateau including Mount Pahnes.

The Samaria Gorge offers the best-known walk on the island but is very much a tourist attraction and offers none of the isolation of the surrounding hills. (See Natural Parks section).

# Other Places of Interest

**Allied War Cemetery**
Souda

**German War Cemetery**
Maleme

**Fortezza, Rethimnon**
Café
Open: Tuesday to Friday 8am-8pm.
Closed Monday, Saturday, Sunday.

**Iraklion Market**
Produce market
Open: Monday to Saturday 8am-8.30pm.

**Kazantzakis' Grave, Iraklion**
Martinegro Bastion.

**Koules Fort, Iraklion**
Open: Summer daily 9am-1pm and 3pm-7pm.

**Venizelos Graves**
Near Hania

# Natural Parks and Places of Interest

**Lasithi Plateau**
Plateau at 850m (2,790ft)
Villages, windmills and Psychro Cave.

**Nidha Plateau and Mount Ida**
Plateau at 1,300m (4,264ft) and highest mountain in Crete.

**Omalos Plateau and Samaria Gorge**
Longest gorge in Europe.
Tourist pavilion at head of gorge; organised trips from all over the island. Bus and boat connections. Public buses leave Hania at 6am, 8.30am, 9.30am and 4.30pm. The journey to the head of the gorge takes $1^1/_2$ hours. The walk should take 5 to 7 hours. There are four boats a day from Ayia Roumeli (the end of the walk. The last boat with a guaranteed bus connection leaves at 5pm. Buses wait for the boats at Hora Sfakion and then return to Hania.The gorge is open May to October. Bus and boat services are less frequent in low season.

**Theriso Gorge**
Narrow gorge near Hania

**Lake Kournas**
Near Georgioupolis
160 acre lake, pedaloes, tavernas.

# Islands

**Ayii Theodori**
Sanctuary for kri-kri goat.

**Elafonisi**
Beautiful beach
Boat trips from Paleohora or
accessible by road.

**Gavdos**
Boat trips from Hora Sfakion.

**Gramvousa**
Venetian fort
No scheduled boat trips; private
excursions possible.

**Hrissi (Goudouronisi)**
Unspoiled beaches
Boat trips from Ierapetra.

**Mohlos**
Archaeological site.

**Psira**
Archaeological site and sanctuary
for kri-kri goat.
Boat trips from Ayios Nikolaos.

**Spinalonga**
Venetian fortress and a leper
colony until 1957
Boat trips from Elounda and Ayios
Nikolaos.

Longer trips are also possible to the
volcanic island of Thera (Santorini).

# Sport

**Climbing**
See mountain section for information on walks and climbing.

**Horseriding**
Horseriding is possible at a riding
school at Amnissos (☎ 081 282005).
It pays to check your health insurance before leaving to confirm that
you have adequate cover.

**Snorkelling**
Snorkelling is a common pursuit
with equipment on sale in resorts;
some snorkellers take spear guns in
order to catch fish. Other opportu-
nites include looking for underwater ruins. There may be possibilities
for scuba diving but there are no
recognised groups or schools.

**Swimming**
Swimming is the easiest sport to
enjoy while on the island. Generally the coastline is very safe,
although extra care should be
taken when the strong summer
winds produce large waves and
occasionally underwater currents.
Few beaches have lifeguards.

**Tennis**
Some hotels have their own tennis
courts and there are clubs in
Iraklion; Beaufort Avenue
☎ 081 226152 and Hania; Dimokratias Avenue ☎ 0821 21293

**Water sports**
Water sports are the main attraction for tourists with many of the

beaches in tourist areas offering windsurfing, waterskiing and even parascending.

# Tourist Offices

*In Crete*
**Ayios Nikolaos**
20 Akti I Koundourou
Information and exchange office.
☎ 0841 22357

**Hania**
6 Akti Tombazi (in the mosque of the Janissaries)
Information and exchange office.
Open: Monday to Saturday 8.30am-2pm, 3-8.30pm.
Closed Sunday.
☎ 081 26426

**Ierapetra**
Kothiri Street
Information office.
Open: Monday to Friday 9am-9pm.
Saturday and Sunday 9am-1pm, 4-8pm.
☎ 0842 28658

**Iraklion**
1 Xanthoudidou Street
Open: Monday to Friday 8am-6pm, Saturday 8am-2pm.
Closed Sunday.
☎ 081 228203/228225

**Rethimnon**
El Venizelou Avenue
Open: Monday to Friday 9am-4.30pm. Saturday and Sunday 9am-2pm.
☎ 0831 29148

**Sitia**
Iroon Polytechniuou Square
Open: Monday to Friday 9am-8pm.
Saturday, Sunday 9am-3pm.
☎ 0843 24955

Other offices claiming to be tourist offices are in fact travel agencies who organise tours and excursions. They can, however, be a useful source of local information and often have exchange counters.

# Useful Addresses

**Association of Greek Camping**
102 Solonos Street
10680 Athens
☎ 3621560

**British Consulate**
16 Odhos Papalaxandrou
☎ 081 224012

**British Embassy**
1 Ploutarhou
Kolonaki
Athens
☎ 736211

**ELPA (Automobile Club of Greece)**
Athens Tower
Messogion 2
Athens

**Greek Travel Office**
2 Amerikis Street
Athens
☎ 01 3223111

**Greek Youth Hostel Association**
4 Dragatsianou Street
Athens
☎ 3234107 or 3237590

**Olympic Airlines**
164 Picadilly
London W1
☎ 081 846 9080

**US Embassy**
91 Leoforosas Sofias
11521 Athens
☎ 721951

## Youth Hostels

Youth hostels on Crete are
generally relaxed, an international
hostel card is not always necessary.
Facilities may be somewhat
primitive but they usually offer
cheap meals and/or kitchen
facilities.

**Ayios Nikolaos**
3 Odhos Stratigou Koraka

80 beds, cooking facilities.
☎ 0841 22823

**Hania**
33 Drakonianou Street
70 beds
☎ 0821 53565

**Malia**
35 beds
☎ 081 285075

**Mirthios**
60 beds
☎ 0832 31202

**Plakias**
50 beds
☎ 0832 31202

**Rethimnon**
Pavlou Vlastou street
46 beds
☎ 0831 22848

**Sitia**
4 Therisou Street
80 beds
☎ 0843 22693

## History of Crete

| DATES | PERIOD | SITES |
|---|---|---|
| 6000BC | Neolithic | Cave of Eileithyia, Knossos, Phaestos, Trapeza Cave |
| 3000-1900BC | Pre- Palatial Early Minoan | Mohlos Vasiliki, Mirtos |
| 1900-1700BC | Palatial Middle Minoan | Knossos, Phaestos Malia, Zakros Old Palaces |

| DATES | PERIOD | SITES |
|---|---|---|
| 1700-1450BC | Late Minoan | Knossos, Phaestos<br>Malia, Zakros<br>New Palaces |
| 1450BC | Great catastrophe | |
| 1450-1100BC | Post-Palatial | |
| 1100-67BC | Mycenea<br>Doric<br>Classical Greek | Numerous city states<br>eg; Dreros, Lato, Itanos |
| 67BC-824AD | Roman | Gortyn |
| 824-961 | Saracen/Arab | Iraklion defensive ditch |
| 961-1204 | Byzantine | Numerous churches |
| 1204-1669 | Venetian | Rethimnon, Hania<br>Iraklion harbours.<br>Frangokastello |
| 1669-1898 | Turkish | Mosques in Rethimnon and<br>Hania |
| 1898-1913 | Rule by the Great powers | |
| 1913 | *Enosis* (union with Greece) | |
| 1941 | Battle of Crete | War cemeteries at Souda and<br>Maleme |

There is no absolute chronology regarding the early period of the island's history, dates given are the most widely accepted ones.

# INDEX

## A

Agiroupoli (Argyrou-
  poli) 164
*Ahladia 50*
Akrotiri (Santorini) 95
Akrotiri Peninsula
  164, 168, 169, 172-3,
  174, 180, 185
Alikianou 197, 202
Almyrida 168, 235
Amari 148, 157
Amari Valley 10, 129,
  147-9, 157
*Amnissos 17, 61, 84, 92,
  235*
Analipsi 49, 50
Anatoli 48
Anemospilia 27
*Anemospilia 104-5*
Angarathos Monas-
  tery (Mirtia) 106
Ano Paleokastro 192,
  193
Ano Viannos 55
Anopoli 159-60
Anoyia 128-9, 133
*Aptera 168, 169, 172,
  233*
Aradena 160
Aradena Gorge 160

Archaeological
  Museum (Ayios
  Nikolaos) 69, 71, 73,
  243
Archaeological
  Museum (Hania)
  177, 182-4, 243
Archaeological
  Museum (Ierapetra)
  52, 243
Archaeological
  Museum (Iraklion)
  17, 44, 57, 60, 71, 78,
  80-85, 92, 93, 116,
  118, 129, 149, 243
Archaeological
  Museum (Re-
  thimnon) 140
Archaeological
  Museum (Sitia) 42,
  44, 244
Arhanes 28, 82, 104,
  105, 117
Arimondi Fountain
  (Rethimnon) 140,
  145
*Arkades 107*
Arkalohori 107
Arkhadi Monastery
  33, 133-4, 239

Arkouditissa Cave of
  Artemis (near
  Katholiko Monas-
  tery) 173
Armeni 50
Arsenali (Iraklion) 88,
  93
Arvi 49, 53, 55, 235
Asigonia 165, 169
Askifou 157, 161
Asomatos 105
*Axos 125, 130*
Ayia Deka 109, 112,
  113
Ayia Ekaterini Church
  (Iraklion) 77, 89, 93,
  239
Ayia Galini 10, 109,
  117, 121, 135, 147,
  149, 152, 235, 238
Ayia Marina 187, 238
Ayia Meronas 108, 117
Ayia Pelayia 124-5,
  133, 235
Ayia Photia 44, 69
Ayia Roumeli 24, 159,
  160, 161, 200, 201,
  205, 244
Ayia Sophia Cave 196
*Ayia Triadha 17, 82, 84,
  117-8, 120, 233*

Ayia Triadha Monastery (Akrotiri Peninsula) 169, 172
Ayia Varvara 108-9
Ayii Theodori 187-8, 246
Ayios Constandinos 63
Ayios Ioannis 149, 160
Ayios Ioannis Church (Rodopou Peninsula) 190-1
Ayios Markos Church (Iraklion) 77, 86, 93
Ayios Mikhail Archangelos (Asomatos) 105
Ayios Minas Cathedral (Iraklion) 89, 93
Ayios Nikolaos 11, 19, 36, 56, 68-9, 71-2, 73, 75, 244, 247, 248
Ayios Nikolaos Church (Hania) 184
Ayios Titos Church (Iraklion) 77, 87-8, 93, 239
Ayios Yeorgios 63, 243

**B**
Bali 125-6, 133, 235
Bembo Fountain (Iraklion) 86

**C**
Castel Selino (Paleohora) 205
City Walls (Iraklion) 89-90, 93

**D**
Danoni (Damnoni) 153
Dikte Range 12, 36
*Diktynnaion 189, 190*

Dimarcheon (Iraklion) 87
Drapanias 191
Drapanos Cape 166
*Dreros 66, 233, 249*

**E**
Eastern Crete 36-55
Eileithyia Cave 56-7, 238, 248
El Greco 19, 77, 86, 125, 133
El Greco Park (Iraklion) 86
Elafonisi 9, 193, 196, 205, 235, 246
*Eleutherna (Eleftherné) 132*
Elos 196
Elounda 66-7, 68, 69, 73
*Elyros 204*
Episkopi 49, 52, 164, 165
*Eteia 41, 50*

**F**
*Falasarna 9, 192-3, 235*
Faneromeni Monastery (near Gournia) 37, 40
Firkas (Hania) 177, 181, 185
Floria 204
Fodhele 19, 125, 133
Folklore Museum (Sitia) 42
Fortezza, Rethimnon 136, 137, 139, 145, 245
Fourfouras 148, 245
Fourni 66
Frangokastello 156, 157, 249

**G**
Gaidouronisi (Donkey Island) 53, 246
Garazo 130
Gavdhos Island 207, 246
Georgioupolis 165, 169, 235, 245
Gerani 164, 169, 235
Gergeri 109
German War Cemetery (Maleme) 188, 189, 245, 249
*Gortyn 11, 22, 29, 96, 112-3, 114, 117, 233, 249*
Goudhouras 49, 50
Gournes 57
*Gournia 25, 37, 41, 233*
Gouverneto Monastery (Akrotiri Peninsula) 169, 172-3, 239
Gramvousa Peninsula 9, 192

**H**
Halidon (Hania) 177, 180, 182
Handras 50
Hania 9, 13, 31, 135, 174-85, 187, 188, 196, 198, 200, 202, 235, 247, 248, 249
Hersonissos 56, 58, 61, 235
Historical and Ethnographical Museum (Iraklion) 88-9, 93, 244
Historical Museum (Hania) 177, 184-5, 243
Hondros 55
Hora Sfakion 156-7, 159, 160, 200, 201, 244

Hrisopigi Monastery (Mournies) 197
Hrisoskalitissa Monastery (Kefali) 193, 196, 239

**I**
Ida (Mountain) 12, 109, 129-30, 245
Ida (Psiloritis) Range 10, 12, 124, 244-5
Ida Cave 129, 133, 239
Ierapetra 9, 49, 52-3, 236, 238, 247
Imbros Ravine 161
Iouktas (Mountain) 22, 105, 117
Iraklion 9, 11, 19, 30, 32, 42, 56, 76-95, 108, 124, 135, 238, 245, 247
Iron Gates/Sidheresportes (Samaria Gorge) 201
Istro 36-7, 41, 48
Itanos (Beach) 45, 46, 236
Izzedine 168

**J**
Janissaries, Mosque of (Hania) 177, 181

**K**
Kakodiki Region 204-5
Kalamafka 48
Kalathas 172
Kali Limines 9, 114-5
Kalithes 205
Kalives 168, 236
Kalo Khorio 48
Kaloudiana 196
Kamares 109, 117, 130, 245
Kamares Cave 109, 117, 129, 130, 239

Kambos 193, 196
Kandanos 204, 207
Kanevaro 181
Kapsa Monastery 49, 50
Kardiotissa Convent (Kera) 62
*Karphi 29, 63*
Kastelli (Hania) 174, 177, 180, 181
Kastelli (near Neapolis) 66, 107
Kastelli (near Thrapsano) 107, 117
Kastelli Kisamou 191-2, 193
Katholiko Monastery (Akrotiri Peninsula) 169, 173
Kato Gouves 57, 61
Kato Zakros 46
Kavousi 39
Kazantzakis, Nikos 20, 89, 90, 92
  Grave of 90, 93, 245
  Museum (Mirtia) 106, 244
Kefali 193, 196
Kera 62
Keratokambos 49, 55
Khameizi 40
*Knossos 11, 17-18, 24, 25, 27-8, 35, 47, 76, 80, 81, 82, 83, 84, 85, 92, 93, 96-102, 104, 112, 116, 233, 248, 249*
Kokkino Hani 57
Kokkino Horio 166
Kokkino Pirgos 121, 236
Kolimvari 189, 191, 236
*Kommos 120*
Kournas, Lake 165, 169, 245
Krasi 62, 65

Kritsa 72, 73, 75, 244
Kritsa Gorge 72
Kutaliko (Kurtalioti) Ravine 152, 153

**L**
Lakki 197, 205
Lasithi Plateau 12, 29, 32, 61-4, 65, 129, 245
*Lato 68, 72-3, 75, 233, 249*
Leben 114
Lendas 113, 117, 236
Levka Ori Mountains 9, 12, 160, 187, 245
*Lissos 204, 205*
Lithines 50
Loggia 86-7, 93
Loutro 9, 157, 159, 160
*Lyttos 107*

**M**
Makrigialos 49, 50, 71, 236
Maleme 33, 35, 176, 188, 189, 249
*Malia (Palace) 60, 61, 233-4, 248, 249*
Malia 25, 56, 58, 60, 61, 64, 236, 248
*Malla 48*
Marathos 125
Margarites 132
Martinegro Bastion (Iraklion) 90
Matala (Beach) 117, 120-1, 236, 238
Maza 207
Melidoni 132
Melidoni Cave 132, 133, 239
Merabello, Gulf of 39, 41, 68
Meronas 149, 157
Meskla 196, 197
Messara Plain 10, 12, 55, 96, 108

Milatos 64-5, 73
*Minoa 172*
Mirsini 40
Mirtia 106
*Mirtos 25, 248*
Mirtos 49, 53, 236
*Mohlos 40, 41, 44, 71, 236, 246, 248*
Mohos 62, 65
Monastaraki Gorge 49
Moni Gonia (Kolimvari) 189-90, 239
Morosini Fountain (Iraklion) 86, 93
Mouliana 40
Mournies 197
Mylopotamus River 131

**N**
Naval Museum (Hania) 177, 181, 243
Nea Mirtos 53
Neapolis 63, 65-6, 73
Nerantzes Djani Minaret (Re-thimnon) 140-1, 145
Nidha Plateau 12, 129, 245
*Nirou Hani (Nirou Megaron)* 57, 61, 82

**O**
Odhos 25 Avgostou (Iraklion) 88
Odhos 1866 (Iraklion) 78, 86, 93
Odhos Lithinon (Hania) 181
Old City (Hania) 180
*Olous 71, 73*
Omalos 197, 202
Omalos Plateau 12, 205, 245

Osia Maria Church (Samaria) 201

**P**
Pachia Amnos 36, 37, 39, 48, 49, 236, 238
Pahnes (Mountain) 12, 160, 197, 245
Paleohora 188, 202, 204, 205, 207, 236, 238
Paleokastro 44, 45, 46, 83
Panayia Kera Church (near Ayios Nikolaos) 19, 72, 73, 240
Panormos 126, 236
Perama 130-2
*Phaestos 11, 25, 35, 81, 82, 96, 115-7, 118, 120, 234, 248, 249*
*Phornou Korphi 53*
*Phourni 104*
Pigi 107
*Pirgos 53*
Plaka (Drapanos Cape) 166
Plaka 68, 73, 236
Plakias 10, 135, 153, 157, 236, 248
Platanias 185, 188, 189, 236
Platanos 39, 41, 192, 193
Plateia 1821 (Hania) 177, 184
Plateia Eleftherias (Iraklion) 78, 79-80, 93
Plateia Kornarou (Iraklion) 85-6, 93
Plateia Tessaron Martyron (Re-thimnon) 144, 145
Plateia Venizelou 86, 93

*Polyrinia 192, 193*
Porta Guova (Re-thimnon) 144, 145
Potamies 61
*Presos (Praesos) 50*
Preveli 152
Preveli Beach 152-3, 157, 236
Preveli Monastery 152, 157, 240
Prines 132
Psira Island 39-40, 44, 246
Psychro 63
Psychro/Diktean Cave 63-4, 65, 129, 239
Public Gardens (Iraklion) 80
Public Gardens (Rethimnon) 144

**R**
Rethimnon 9, 32, 126, 135-45, 147, 164, 236, 237, 238, 247, 248, 249
*Rhizenia 108*
Rocca Al Mare Fortress (Iraklion) 88, 93
Rodopou Peninsula 9, 189-91
Rodovani 202, 204, 207
Rogdia 124

**S**
Samaria 201
Samaria Gorge 9, 12, 16, 156, 159, 197, 198, 200-1, 205, 245
San Francisco Church (Hania) 177, 182-3
San Francisco Church (Rethimnon) 141, 144

Santorini (Thera) 17, 28, 47, 53, 68, 85, 92, 95, 246
Seli Ambelou Pass (Lasithi Plateau) 62, 65
Sfakia 187-207
Sfinari 193
Shiavo Bastion (Hania) 181
*Sibyrita 148*
Sisi 64, 238
Sitia 9, 11, 36, 40, 41-2, 44, 49, 236, 247, 248
Sitia Range 12, 36
*Sklavokampos 128*
Skotino Cave 57
Skridlof (Hania) 177, 184
Souda 9, 35, 168, 169, 172, 180
Souda Bay 9, 164, 168, 174
Souda War Cemetery 169, 172, 245, 249
Souyia 202, 204, 205, 207, 236
Spili 149, 152, 157
Spinalonga 11, 66-8, 73, 246
Stalis (Stalidas) 58, 61
Stavros 169, 172, 236

**T**
Tarraios, River 200
Tavronitis 188-9, 202, 204
Theriso 196
Theriso Gorge 196, 205, 245
Thira 95
Thrapsano 106, 107
Thronos 148
*Tilissos 128, 133, 234*
Toplou Monastery 19, 44-5, 46, 240
Trapeza (Kronos) Cave 63, 248
Triymartyri Cathedral (Hania) 184
Tzermadion 63, 65

**V**
Vai (Beach) 45, 46, 236
Valsamonero Monastery (Vorizia) 109, 117
Vamos 166
*Vasiliki 25, 49, 248*
Vathipetro 20, 105-6, 117
Venetian Harbour (Hania) 177, 180, 249
Venetian Harbour (Rethimnon) 140, 145, 249

Venizelos Graves 169, 172, 185, 245
Venizelos, Eleftherios 33, 80, 169, 172, 176, 184, 185, 196
Vizari 148
Voni 106
Vorizia 109
Voulismeni, Lake 69
Vrisses 161, 166
Vrondisi Monastery (Zaros) 89, 109, 117, 240

**W**
Western Crete 187-207

**X**
Xerokambos 48
Xiloskalo 197, 200

**Y**
Yerakari 149

**Z**
*Zakros 11, 25, 28, 35, 44, 45-8, 82, 234, 236, 248, 249*
Zambeliou (Hania) 177, 181
Zaros 109
Ziros 50
*Zou 50*

## A Note to the Reader

We hope you have found this book informative, helpful
and enjoyable. It is always our aim to make our
publications as accurate and up to date as possible.
With this in mind, we would appreciate any comments
that you might have. If you come across any information to update this book or discover something new
about the area we have covered, please let us know so
that your notes may be incorporated in future editions.

As it is MPC's principal aim to keep our publications lively and responsive to change, any information
that readers provide will be a valuable asset to us in
maintaining the highest possible standards for our
books.

Please write to:
Senior Editor
Moorland Publishing Co Ltd
Free Post
Ashbourne
Derbyshire
DE6 9BR